INTERNAL COMBUSTION

INTERNAL COMBUSTION

A LOVE STORY

TOM MORTON

MAINSTREAM
PUBLISHING

EDINBURGH AND LONDON

ACKNOWLEDGEMENTS

Thanks to all at Mainstream, especially Deborah Kilpatrick
and, as ever, Bill and Pete

Copyright © Tom Morton, 2000
All rights reserved
The moral right of the author has been asserted

First published in Great Britain in 2000 by
MAINSTREAM PUBLISHING COMPANY (EDINBURGH) LTD
7 Albany Street
Edinburgh EH1 3UG

ISBN 1 84018 340 3

A catalogue record for this book is available from the British Library

Typeset in Stone Print and Univers
Printed and bound in Great Britain by Creative Print and Design, Wales

There is more to a car than the engine.
The Practical Car-Owner, 1956

What the well-dressed car is wearing . . . PORTMAN template-
tailored SEAT COVERS, in Ocelot, Tartans, Repps, Cords,
Moquettes etc. Each set individually tailored with contrasting
piping. Send for our free patterns. Complete sets from 59/6.
Portman advertisement, 1955

When there is no war and no filibustering in South Africa, no
uncharted islands to explore, this land of policemen and accurate
maps and black coats on Sundays is apt to bore certain types of
temperament. The purchase of a motorcycle imparted the spice of
risk and uncertainty and bohemianism into such a life.
Reminiscences of Motorcycling, by IXION, 1920

CONTENTS

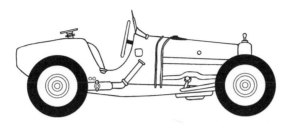

PRE-IGNITION

My father, George Morton, who now drives a Honda CRV, inspired my love affair with cars and, though he probably didn't realise it at the time, motorcycles too. He selflessly allowed his memories to be sifted for the purposes of this book, as well as supplying a 1972 copy of *The Observer's Book of Automobiles* and much hospitality. This book is respectfully and affectionately dedicated to him, and to my late mother, Euphemia MacCalman. Their respective driving and high-volume passengership have been an inspiration throughout my life. Dad taught me everything I know about car repair, including the correct method of kicking a tyre.

The fact that there is, almost unprecedentedly in a Morton publication, no swearing to speak of in *Internal Combustion* will be a matter of some relief to more than just my esteemed paw. Not that Mr Morton Senior has been above deploying the occasional mild epithet in his time behind so many different wheels. I very nearly spared him the incident which caused so much amusement to myself and my sisters, all packed into the back seat and growing rather too big for the small space in a Ford Zodiac Executive, when he began using the word 'poof' as an insult aimed at truck drivers. But then again . . .

'Look at that dirty diesel smoke coming out of his exhaust! What a horrible poof!' he would shout through the windscreen, somewhere on the M6.

'What's wrong?' he demanded as we rolled about in paroxysms of giggledom. 'A poof is a small soft footstool!' He meant it too.

A few small chunks of this book have been reworked from articles previously commissioned by and published in *The Scotsman*, the *Daily Express* and *New Statesman*. Many thanks to the long-suffering editorial executives I have worked with at these august organs, especially Alistair Clark at *The Scotsman*, David Hamilton at the *Express* and Alistair Moffat at *New Statesman Scotland*. Daniel Ford, bless his Rhodesian Ridgeback-chewed leather seats, commissioned the *GQ* assignment which has been mercilessly appropriated and enlarged upon for my own nefarious purposes. In South Africa, Rowan Pelling, Ingrid Rolando and Dave McGregor advised, reassured and pointed me in various directions, some of them right.

Heather Curley, producer of *Wheelnuts* for Scottish Television, gave and is still giving me the opportunity to drive ridiculous machinery, and paying me for the privilege. Justyn Jones at Small World Productions forced me, in the end, to buy the Land Rover. Susan, as ever, pulled me from the metaphorical and literary wreckage time and time again, stitched me up and sent me on my way, even though she had grave misgivings about lots of things. Anne Bates put up with my wanderings and erratic incompetence, and still managed to produce, without fail, a great radio show every week.

As for Magnus, James and Martha, they sit in the back of the Land Rover and demand decent music (Magnus); that I go faster and think about buying a TVR (James); and complain about the smell of damp dog (Martha). I hope their in-car memories prove to be as potent and as pleasurable as mine.

Tom Morton,
Shetland,
June 2000

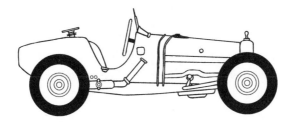

BIG BOYS' TOYS

L ook at you. Just look at you.' My wife had slid to a rattling, gravelly stop in her Toyota Hi-Lux Crew Cab pick-up truck (medical redneck edition), and was now confronting the six male figures gathered outside the house she shares with three of them. Hands on hips, a huge jangle of car keys swinging from her fingers, she would have been threatening if she hadn't been smiling. I felt threatened anyway.

And, really, there was no need. She knew about the Land Rover. She knew about the motorbike. More to the point, she knew me. She had long since sussed the permanent teenager within my forty-something body, and the hopeless machinery addict she had, for worse or for worse, married.

Fortunately, she liked the Land Rover. A 110 County Station Wagon, three years old, with the 300 series TDI diesel engine, Rioja red, full Land Rover service history, the size of a house, the shape of a brick, a vehicle so uncompromisingly itself, it sat, like the final triumph of function over aesthetics, on the shores of the sea-loch we perch and have our being beside.

I loved it, that wheeled metal box; I still do. It is the end of the journey described in this book, the final purchase, the arrival at a destination which dozens of four-wheeled objects have trundled, rasped, careered and skidded me towards during a lifetime measured out in cubic centimetres, 0–60 times, oversteer and understeer. Honest. It is. The infatuation is over. This is true married love. No more sports coupé fantasies or luxury saloon daydreams. I found my mobile grail, and it was made in Solihull, won't go faster than 80 mph, has, instead of air-conditioning, phenomenally old-fashioned metal flaps you open with levers below the flat windscreen, and when faced with a Ferrari or a Lamborghini, will simply lumber right on over it without the slightest pause. It is pure essence, a design half a century old and it is mine, mine, mine. Once the loan's paid off.

'We just came over to have a look at the Land Rover, Susan,' murmurs Chris; neighbour, lawyer and the man currently sitting astride a bright yellow motorcycle.

'And I thought, what the hell, it's a nice day, let's get out the bike,' I mutter, while my two sons, JM and JP, grin and soak with their high-powered water rifles anyone not keeping a watchful eye on them. James, Chris's son, home from his Ph.D in oceanography, has refused a shot on the MZ Skorpion Sport, 660cc of single-cylinder delight, made in the former East Germany from the joint drawing board of British *über*-designers Seymour and Powell.

'I haven't been on a bike for, oh, five years,' says James.

'I haven't been on one for twenty-five years,' says his father, to general laughter, and a queasy eruption in the pit of my stomach.

'Err . . . no more than 4,000 revs, Chris. It's still running in . . .'

My wife purses her lips. She doesn't like the bike.

'And me, I'm just waiting to have a shot,' says Scott, husband of our friend and childminder Elaine, a man reared on early Kawasaki two-stroke water-cooled 'kettles', whose yearning for bikedom is palpable, and who has a vintage 1960s leather jacket carefully stored away at home, festooned with badges and worth a fortune to a posing rock star with a *Wild One* fetish.

'Oh, I suppose I'll just have to leave you to it,' says Susan, marching housewards. 'Big boys' toys, that's all they are. Men! What are they like!'

In fact, Susan is a biker at heart, and it was she who introduced me to the delights of MZ (Motarradwerk Zschopau) when they were still an East German manufacturer of two-stroke singles with an appealingly eccentric character; bikes which smoked and clanged and ring-ting-tinged with a complete disregard for ecology. The Skorpion is different. Japanese engine, solid engineering, pretty as a Ducati at a third of the price. I love it.

Susan doesn't like it; she dislikes all bikes when ridden by me. She fears my injury or death, and with good cause: she bears the scars of two horrible accidents, the last of which ended her motorcycling career. Plus, being a doctor, she can tell all the usual horror stories of bikers skinned alive, stones having to be removed from skin with tweezers and sandpaper, paraplegia a-go-go. And I remember the Harley rider I met, minus a leg and an arm, waiting for the insurance money to come through to customise a bike and sidecar and get back on the road. Grinning, laughing, talking up a storm, a feverish look in his eye.

Anyway, here's the deal, motorcycle-wise: I have two bikes. One is an elderly Triumph TR6, the standard issue police Triumph from the late '60s and early '70s, before the cops discovered BMWs and reliability. It's been tarted up to look like a Bonneville, but it's rusty and in need of serious restoration. It sits in a garage, and every so often I go and look at it. Then I send away for a spare part, and look at that for a while. Every year or so, I fit the spare part, sometimes successfully. It's an investment for the future, I tell my wife. It will be our nest egg in years to come, an appreciating asset. She snorts at this, in a dismissively cynical way. Something she has perfected over the years.

Then there's the MZ, purchased just a few months ago, when the strong pound and an oversupply of bikes meant you could pick up a brand new, old model Skorpion Sport for less than three grand. I have loved the design ever since I saw Seymour and Powell, the fattest bikers in the world outside of American Harley riders' clubs, talking it up on telly. It was a secret from Susan until the day it arrived, and after initially pretending I had it on test, in my capacity as all-round hack and blagger of free services from gullible companies, I was forced to confess all when my daughter Mart demanded to know, in that voice which brooks no dissembling, if I'd bought it. I crumbled like a piece of rhubarb. Crumble.

When Susan returned after the consequent in-the-huff hour or two at her mother's, which, handily for such huffs, is next door, we reached an accommodation: I could keep the bike, if she could have a weed-burner for the garden. She is, you see, as horticulturally obsessed as I am enslaved by machines. And let's face it, a weed-burner offers all sorts of scope for a gadgeteer like myself to have a little fun pretending to be Robert De Niro in *The Deer Hunter* (that bit with the flamethrower). Not, of course, that any decent, right-thinking citizen would imagine being so nasty to dandelions and docks. Not really.

Anyway, I agreed. And peace, for a time, reigned.

I mentioned machinery in general. Now, this is not a book about gadgets, outboard motors, Swiss Army knives, pushbikes (though I own an embarrassing four, including a hand-made Orbit which I get tired just looking at), palmtops, electric garlic presses, tractors (an unfulfilled yearning as yet), cameras (still), cameras (video) or cameras (digital). It is about cars and motorbikes because, of all the machines which have infested my life, these mobility-interfaces have provided more pleasure, have measured out the thrills, spills, loves, lusts, horrors and failures of my life more than any Victorinox 32-blade penknife (though I wouldn't mind that new one with the built-in light, to be frank).

'Be careful, Chris; what on earth will I say to Amelia if . . . ' But Chris has departed down the single-track road in a thumping single-cylinder roar, dust billowing behind him as a quarter of a century of bike-avoidance disappears. The dogs, locked inside the porch, start barking. Sheep scatter. Arctic terns lift off the shingle beach below us in a terrified whirring cloud. A seal pops up for a look. Chris's son watches his father go, his face a mixture of amusement and concern. Susan, meanwhile, is looking at me in a how-long-will-this-mid-life-crisis-go-on-for kind of way.

I'm hoping to keep it trundling along for quite a few years yet. I have already been accused by the managing editor of *The Scotsman* of preserving my male menopause artificially in order to find new subjects to write about; in truth, all I'm trying to do is write about things so I can fund the ongoing emotional crisis itself, and the mechanical expression thereof. I mean, it could be worse. I could be out there in the hideous embarrassment zone of an ageing ran-dan merchant in an ill-advised baseball cap and Timberland sweatshirt, attempting to shag eighteen-year-olds. Divorced dads at discos – is there anything sadder? I have seen *American Beauty*. I know how it ends.

Better to embarrass yourself on board a Ducati, or by changing your car rather too often for comfort. But I don't have a Ducati. I have an MZ. I love it. I don't want a Ducati, not even a 996 SP. No, not even as a gift.

Which takes me back to the Land Rover. I have just dispensed with a perfectly fine, if exceedingly boring, Peugeot 406 turbo diesel saloon for the big beast's sake. Some friends (Chris included) think I am mad, but here are the facts:

(1) We live in a remote corner of the Shetland Islands, along a rough single-track road, and face frequent bouts of weather best described as the overreacting vengeance of God upon sinful humanity.

(2) My wife is a doctor whose Toyota Hi-Lux often breaks down or becomes involved in mysterious collisions with giant sheep, many apparently made of metal, and is thus off the road when an emergency call comes in from a patient with a lobster wedged in one of his less accessible orifices.

(3) I have always loved Land Rovers.

(4) I have, despite always having loved Land Rovers, never owned one.

(5) I regularly have to carry three children, a granny, two dogs, a pig, a few sheep, various bags of animal feed, hay, straw and my own ever-expanding ego, all at the same time. In thick snow and/or mud.

(6) The Peugeot needed a service anyway.

The love affair goes back to Dinky and Corgi and all the rubber-tyred toys small boys were given instead of Sony Playstations in the 1960s. Not that the rubber tyres ever remained attached to the wheels for very long. I specialised in stuffing these tyres up my sister's nose, and my own, on one occasion necessitating a visit to Dr Freedlander to have a complete set

INTERNAL COMBUSTION

of toy VW Beetle tyres removed from four Morton nostrils. It was a relief to reattach them, because while the unpeeling of toy car tyres was in itself very satisfying, the difficulty of rolling the car along on the edges of its metal hubs always left a bad taste in the mouth. And, indeed, a rubbery odour in the nasal passages.

Anyway, I owned a grey Land Rover, a Dinky, and what I now know to have been a Series One 80-inch, possibly Royal Air Force issue. With a plastic imitation canvas top, quickly lost. So, as in many car purchases, the memory of childhood toys has played its part.

Since then, I have driven Land Rovers of every shape and size, from Range Rovers to Discoveries, Air-Portable Lightweights to beefed-up off-road racers. Even the awful Freelanders. All I really wanted was what is now known as the Defender, the boxy, original, off-road slab of aluminium and metal that is the generic Land Rover. And I knew, somehow, that owning one would mark the end of something, the conclusion of all that romantic faffing about with convertibles and tuned, turbo-charged, petrolised, low-slung metal penises with tyres costing £150 apiece. Growing up.

It would, this Land Rover life, be about steadiness, deliberate progress, getting there in the end, rather than pell-mell panting to shave seconds off a journey time. It would be a life where driving was a kind of meditative act: listening, watching (for Land Rovers, due to having a massive separate chassis, can have cabs which resemble greenhouses, they're so light and glassy – conservatories attached to Sherman tanks), having and holding the extended family and various accoutrements, animal, vegetable and mineral.

They're slow, in other words. You don't drive a Land Rover fast. You lumber, rattling and chattering along in that lorryish diesel way. Because you have to have a diesel engine. Of course you do.

Here's why. The official Land Rover handbook gives the factory fuel consumption figures for the V8 petrol engine (no longer available) and the TDI diesel in my vehicle (also no longer available, and replaced by the five-cylinder, very nearly civilised TD5): the diesel will just about top 28 mpg at a steady 56 mph (whoever drives at a steady 56 mph?), while the V8 is quoted at 11 to 14. Which means that on a bad day, with a bit of off-road rough and tumble, you could be getting anything down to 6 mpg.

This is hardly what you would call environmentally friendly. It is hardly economically viable, unless you're an eccentric millionaire. And as someone with a sort of greenish tinge to his life (hey, we collect bottles for the bank, when we remember, turn the weekly tonne of household newspapers into pig bedding, refuse extra poly-bags when shopping, drink local beer; especially, we drink local beer), driving a vehicle which on its own could drain the North Sea of oil in a couple of years seemed unwarrantable.

The diesel, of course, is hardly a Fiat Cinquecento or a Swatch Smart Car, but it is liveable with. And the direct injection diesel is remarkably clean, compared to the horrid old Nissan Patrol we used to own, which belched blue smoke like one of those dodgy trucks in the classic, and only gravel-delivery, sex grudge film *Hell Drivers* (Stanley Baker, Sean Connery, 1950s, brilliant stuff). So we may use the world's resources rather quickly, but we do it without creating too much dirt. Or try not to.

And the Land Rover will last. Possibly for ever. Martin, who runs the local dealership, told me that a tin of WD40 would 'keep the edges looking fresh'. And it's the edges which will go or, to be precise, it's the places where the rust-free aluminium panels interface with steel screws. Nobody seems to have told Land Rover about electrolysis, which I was taught about at school and which dictates that the presence of a slower-corroding metal in contact with a faster-corroding one will make the faster one corrode, well, even faster, if you see what I mean. And this has nothing to do with hair removal from women at vast expense. Or men, for that matter. Hence glittering 110s such as mine with nasty brown screws keeping the doors attached.

'My dad had one.' Chris has returned from his flirtation with bikerdom safely and is regarding the red 110 thoughtfully. 'It was virtually the first car I was allowed to drive on my own, battering in and out to Lerwick. The half shafts used to slide in and out, so you would actually see the wheel moving outwards gradually, until it eventually spun off and the hub hit the tarmac. I presume,' he turned to me, 'they've fixed that.'

They have. At least, I think they have. I presume.

At any rate, as I write, I am satisfied – I am happy, I am complete, in terms of my motorisation. I wish no further trade-ins, merely a long-term service relationship with Martin at the Bixter Garage. We shall grow old together, my Land Rover and I. And there will be fun. There will be mud-plugging and off-roading. There will be (and Susan hasn't realised this yet) a host of extras. I have the magazines. I know about the range of alloy wheels, the spotlights, the intercoolers, the seat covers, spun aluminium protective panels, even the 6.2-litre replacement V8 GMC diesels . . .

And there is the MZ, too, the last motorbike I will buy. The Triumph to tinker with, an eternal 'winter project'; the MZ to run whenever weather allows and frugality dictates that a wallet-sapping journey in the Land Rover is unnecessary.

This book is the story of how I reached this point in my life, the journey to enlightenment, to peace, to an ability to (just about) avoid *Auto Trader* on the newsagent's shelves, and to drive past a BMW dealer or a motorbike shop without turning my head. It includes, explicitly, a journey through part of Africa, and, implicitly, a lifetime's driving through Europe, America and especially Britain, this tiny country.

From caravans to superbikes, TV antics and journalistic frolics, through back-seat lust and industrial tragedy, it is a love story, and the passion described is one I think that millions of us share.

And if even a small fraction of that number – I'll settle for, oh, say one 25th of several million; more if you insist – buy this book, I might be able to afford a Ducati and a Ferrari as well as the Land Rover, the MZ and the Triumph. Not that I would spend the money in that way, of course. As I've said, my automotive dreams have ended.

No. I'd definitely buy a Vincent Black Lightning. Or perhaps a Brough Superior. And a couple of Astons, of course.

Consistency was never my strong point.

PART ONE

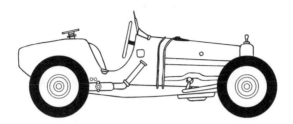

MR GREAT BIG CHICKEN DUCK

'S TOP THIS CAR RIGHT NOW AND LET ME OUT!' It was a clenched-teeth, reined-in roar, accompanied by the dull, papery *AA Book of the Road* being slammed shut with a dull, papery boom. My mother's face set into a granite glare, and my father accelerated. Not much, but slightly. Annoyingly.

He shook his heavily Brylcreemed head. 'I KNEW we should have gone first left at that last roundabout!' The car's speed increased as Dad's desperation to right our geographical displacement grew.

Mum, meanwhile, was breathing heavily. 'YOU were the one who insisted on coming off the dual carriageway and going cross-country in the first place. Now LET ME OUT THIS MINUTE! PULL OVER!'

'Mummy, can I tell you a joke?'

'NOT NOW, TOMMY!' On the back parcel shelf, one sister was sound asleep beneath a red velvet coat, occasional rubbery slurps coming from her pink plastic dummy teat, while down in the depths of the Wolseley's floor, wrapped around the prop shaft tunnel, my other sister was squirming and gulping, preparing to howl in response to the tension emanating from the front seats. It was dawn, somewhere in the pre-motorway midlands of England, and we had been driving all night.

'But, Mummy, did you hear about the policeman who was driving beside this car and he said to the driver, pull over, and the driver said, no, it's a cardigan?' A pause. The whirring, whining thrum of the engine and transmission, that wildly exciting aroma of travel – leather, petrol, exhaust fumes, baby sickness, Tweed perfume, hair oil and Old Spice aftershave. The draggy, prickly sense of wakefulness after a night's motorised movement.

And then the snort of my mother's suppressed laughter erupting, and Dad's hissing giggle as a garage appeared on the left, and we slowed to pull in and, against every impulse in my father's bones, ask directions. The dull, empty silence as the engine was switched off, followed by the ticking and clicking of the car cooling down. And Mum and Dad holding hands, embracing, kissing, even. Did they kiss? I'm sure they did.

'Can I go to the toilet, Mum?'

'Yes, dear, if the garage has one.' Because sometimes they didn't, back in the 1960s. Sometimes they did, and made you buy petrol before you were allowed to borrow the greasy key and enter some shit-festooned pit of the damned. And then my sister's wee voice from down below my feet, happy, proud.

'Mummy, I don't need the toilet.'

'That's good, dear.'

'Because, Mummy, you know something?'

'What's that, dear?'

'I've already been.'

'Aaaaarrrghhh!' Dad was leaping from the car, in a slamming of heavy metal, as the aromatic proof of overnight peeing began to seep up from the blue-tufted carpets of Dad's beloved Wolseley 6/110 Mk II. And I smiled, because at least it wasn't me. At least I'd made them laugh. And we were on holiday, moving in mysterious unexplored territory, driving all night, feeling that almost unbearable joy of movement, of uncertainty, of looming strangeness. A sisterly pee was a small price to pay. Especially because she was going to be doing the paying, in the form of ignominious pant-peeling and parental disapproval. Through the windscreen I could see Dad coming back with a borrowed bucket, ready to rid his pride and joy of childish bodily fluids.

Because Dad loved that Wolseley. So did I. It was the first car I ever drove, balanced on Dad's lap, my hands on the wheel as he navigated the big two-tone blue beast around Glasgow. But I preferred blowing the horn, which involved pressing a semi-circular chromium bar within the wheel's circumference. And, to be honest, even more satisfying was sitting on the front passenger seat, alone with my father, slithering tiny on the polished blue leather, in those unbelted days. Now you can probably be jailed for letting your child sit on your knee as you drive, and the idea of babies asleep on parcel shelves or wrapped in blankets on the floor is anathema in our safety-conscious society. But we travelled thousands of miles that way, and never came to the slightest harm. I don't even remember being hurled forward by any hard braking. I just remember how great it was to move.

The Wolseley, Dad has told me since, was second hand, but it was the biggest, newest, most expensive vehicle he had ever owned in his youthful life. He would have been in his late twenties. By the time he acquired it, the three-litre, six-cylinder engine had already been replaced once, but I don't recall anything about its mechanics. It is the leather and walnut of the interior that stays with me. That and the fact that my mother was scared of its glinting grandeur.

It was huge, you see, compared to the car she had learned to drive in and still used. A Fiat 600; tinny, plasticky, a dark, cheap blue. It smelled not of leather but of over-heated cardboard and glue, like something not quite finished. Its engine didn't make that restrained, heavy, slow Wolseley growl. It chattered and pitter-pattered like a sort of mild mechanical fart.

One day, a Sunday, dressed in her best Gospel Hall clothes, Mum had to use the Wolseley to go hospital visiting. Some elderly relative was ensconced in Hairmyres, an old fever hospital in East Kilbride. I went with her, dressed in a hideous short-trousered tweed suit which chafed my thighs, and in a mood to be scathingly critical of her driving abilities. Compared to Dad, after all, she was only a woman. And I knew that women drivers were all dangerous terrors, to be treated with fear and extreme caution.

INTERNAL COMBUSTION

All went well until we reached the Hairmyres car park, where Mum, unaccustomed to the long nose of the Wolseley, drove it into a brick wall. There was a great clangy splintering of glass and the amazingly loud crackle and thump of impacting metal. I was shocked. My mother was distraught. Tears streaming down her face, she tottered out of the car to examine the damage. A passing gardener tried to comfort her. 'Don't worry, hen,' he said, 'your father'll understand.'

I looked at him as if he was mad. This man seriously thought my mother was young enough to have a father? I had heard tales of my grandad, but he had been dead for centuries. And my mother, she was old. Ancient. Beyond time. Not as old as my dad, though, who, when he found out about this Wolseley-bashing incident, would rage, I knew, with a terrifying explosive fury which would die away into a quiet anger and then peaceful acceptance within minutes of hearing the bad, bad news.

Mum and I examined the broken spotlights and twisted bumper, and I wondered how on earth it would ever be fixed, how metal could be unbent, glass stuck together. It seemed like perfection had been unmade, and could never be restored.

But that was what happened when you let women drive big cars.

And now my wife is screaming at me.

'STOP THIS BLOODY CAR RIGHT NOW,' she is bellowing at the tinted glass: we're in a Nissan Patrol somewhere in Normandy, with three children in the back safely belted in, two of them absorbed in Nintendo Gameboys, one dribblingly asleep.

'STOP THE CAR AND FIND YOUR OWN WAY IF YOU'RE SO BLOODY CLEVER!' I shake my head from side to side, gelled, spiky hair quivering. It was that era. I was that fashion victim. 'Women can't read maps. Just like they can't park. It's a left side, right side of the brain thing. You can't help it.'

'SHUT UP!'

'I mean, I don't mind driving around here all day. It's scenic, after all, isn't it? The Battlefields of the Second World War Grand Bloody Tour. And the firs. And the Bloody Napoleonic . . .'

'If you'd asked, if you'd only just stopped to ask at that service area, we would have found the campsite ages ago.'

'If you'd ever learned to read a map . . .'

'I was a Queen's Guide, I'll have you know! I got my Duke of Edinburgh's Gold . . .'

'Daddy? Mummy?' It's JM in the back seat, his battle with Tetris temporarily suspended. 'Listen to this. Knock knock.'

'Who's there?' his two parents reply in unison, automatically, hostilities suspended.

'Mister.'

'Mister Who?'

'Mister Great Big Chicken Duck.'

JM waits for a reaction. And we laugh, bickering defused, and although I don't reach over and grab her hand, I might have, could well have if I was that kind of affectionate, demonstrative type. JM is smiling, his mum and dad are breathing more easily as the big diesel engine clatters and coughs us along a poplar-lined road leading us God alone knows where. And who cares? Not us. We're on holiday, after all.

'Tom?'

'Yes, dear?'

'Slow down a bit.'

A gnarly, vicious, cramping rage grips my sentimental old heart and snaps off the sunshine; hatred wells up within me. 'I AM NOT GOING FAST! WE'RE QUITE SAFE! YOU'RE THE ONE WHO HAS ALL THE ACCIDENTS!'

This is unarguably true, but still deliberately provocative and unfair. Soon we will be on to the scientifically proven inabilities of the female in the realms of spatial awareness, making for terrible reversing incidents (such as the BMW 520 that Susan once reduced to a scratched, trimless hulk by backing it through a hedge), and then I begin to wonder what it would be like if I did stop the car and let her out, and she did walk off, away into the fields and hedgerows of France. Once, we were on holiday in Provence, Dad and Mum and me and my sisters, and we had paired up with another family from Scotland. We were in a too-small Fiat 125, all red plastic and rusty seams. They were in front of us and suddenly their Humber Sceptre – the Hillman Hunter one, with the walnut dashboard, vinyl roof and fake plastic basketwork seats – slid to a halt on the hard shoulder. We swerved past and then pulled in, all craning back to see what had happened. And there was Auntie Edith, stamping off into the corn by the side of the road, determined, moving with real intention. Nobody said anything. This was what had been threatened in our family travels and travails many, many times, but had never actually happened. We were stunned.

After a few seconds, Uncle Edwin opened the driver's door of the Sceptre and stood gazing after his wife, his lips moving. We couldn't hear what he was saying, not clearly. It sounded angry, though, not pleading. Their two children remained invisible in the car, but I'm prepared to bet they were howling. And that it was that noise, thin and desperate, not Uncle Edwin's shouted imprecations, which brought Auntie Edith slowly back, arms folded across her chest.

Nobody ever mentioned the incident again.

I ease off on the accelerator of the Nissan and let the throaty, ratchety croak of the big diesel fade a little, so that conversation is almost possible at a civilised level.

'Sorry,' I say, 'soon be there. Everybody's a bit tetchy.'

'We'll only get there if you turn back.'

'Knock, knock!' says Magnus.

'Mummy! I've done a poo!' says James.

The first words I ever spoke, according to family legend, were 'Tiumf Enown', my lisping, gummy, toothless attempt on my father's then pride and joy, a Triumph Renown. For years, I would quiz Dad about this car, which he dearly loved, despite its deathtrap rustiness. It had an iconic status within my life. First words. And my father's first passionate relationship with a motor.

'It was absolutely beautiful,' he would say, a faraway glint in his eye. 'Razor-edged styling, and sporty.' He had acquired it, just after I was born, in 1956, having passed his test during his national service in the RAF. He cannot now recall much about the battered old Singer he took that test in, in Norwich, but I can. It was an open-topped sports car with a crash gearbox, terrible brakes and a terrified examiner squashed in next to my dashing young dad, whiplash thin and dressed in his flight-lieutenant's uniform. All these details are lodged firmly in my mind, though my father says that it was a saloon, and he can't remember what kind of gearbox it was. But I know.

Ah, how I loved the idea of my father tearing up the roads and lanes of Norfolk in an ancient, rackety old two-seater. I adored the idea that he was once a flight-lieutenant, an intrepid pilot, rakish warrior of the skies . . .

But the truth was that Dad had trained as a dentist and served his time in the RAF pulling and filling teeth. If you were a dentist, you automatically gained the rank of flight-lieutenant. This, and the fact that he was far too young to have been in the war, was a source of grave disappointment to me. But at least he had once owned a rattly old sports car, and had lived a romantic idyll with my mum, far from their working-class, deeply religious upbringing among the dark satanic mills of Central Steelworks, Lanarkshire.

But then I came along. And the Singer had to go, replaced by the Triumph Renown, which stayed around just long enough for me to learn, roughly, how to say its name.

I look at a picture of a Triumph Renown now in the *I Spy Automobiles* paperback before me, and I see a reserved, slightly cynical face, superior, sort of upper class. In those days all cars had faces. Headlight eyes, radiator-grille noses and bumper mouths. Now, the advent of tiny corner halogen lamps, non-existent air intakes and unchromed bumpers has wiped the expression from motor vehicles. They're all inert, lifeless, mere machines compared to the anthropomorphic vitality of my childhood's cars. The Morris Cowley which came after the Renown looked completely gormless and stupid, like Billy Bunter. The Vauxhall Velox was a cheapskate Flash Harry, well above its station in life. Look at a Toyota Carina CDX sitting in a motorway service area, or an Avensis or a Mondeo, and what do you see? Metal and glass. Something utterly devoid of personality and life. A machine without any quirks or charm. Sure, you get post-modern fakery like the Jaguar S-Type or the Rover 75, the new Beetle and Mini throwbacks, cynical sentimentalism using imitative styling cues to kindle nostalgia in the buying public. But, with the honourable exception of the Land Rover Defender (even a Jeep Wrangler is a piece of trendified nonsense), they're just tarts in drag.

They work, though, those Toyotas and Fords, Mondeos and Corollas. They have three-year unlimited mileage warranties, six-year anti-corrosion guarantees. CD players, air-conditioning, electric sunroofs at no extra charge – all kinds of things I could never have dreamed of, gazing at the early evening glory of that Wolseley, watching Dad switch the lights on, then off, on then off, as the little cream-and-red badge in the centre of the tall, imperious radiator grille glowed and faded, glowed and faded.

'You can tell when a Wolseley's behind you,' he would say, 'because there's that extra little light between the headlights.' For year after back-seat year, travelling in the drowsy darkness as we made that inevitable midnight run to the Lake District or Torquay, or later France and Spain, I would gaze out at the vehicles left in our wake, and wish there was a Wolseley following, a speck of indistinct light between the glare of dipped beams behind.

Sometimes, I look in the dipping mirror of whatever I happen to be driving, and I still search for that romantic flicker of the past.

I nearly bought a Wolseley 6/110 a couple of years ago. It was the whole classic car syndrome writ large: own the car your dad did, or the car your dad could never afford. Be your dad. Beat your dad. I just loved that Wolseley. I wanted it back. My childhood. Happiness.

So I travelled down to the Borders, somewhere near Langholm, and there it was, the same colour as I remembered. Two-tone blue, with unmarked chrome, restored at God knows what expense. The man whose retirement project it had been had died, and his widow was keen to sell it. She was shaky and distracted, so I dealt with her son, a good ten years younger than me, and rather brusque. To put it mildly.

'It was something he took up in the last five years of his life, doing up old cars,' he said. 'Just liked fiddling around in the garage. Had a Morris Minor before this. It was simpler. This bloody thing took up too much of his energy, I think. Too complicated. Mam says it put him in his grave. Three grand, no offers.'

I opened the door, and waited for that most potent of senses, smell, to take me back to my childhood joys of journeying. But, instead, there was the strong scent of air freshener which could not quite hide a nasty stale animal aroma. The leather seats were crushed and worn, and the lovely gloss of the dashboard walnut had dulled to a mottled grey-brown. It was rippled and lifting in places. The chrome horn bar on the steering wheel was rough and dusted with bubbles of rust. I turned the key, but nothing happened.

'Battery must be flat,' said the son. 'I can get some jump leads.'

'Don't bother,' I said, feeling that draggy, dead feeling in my gut, which meant I was not on any account going to buy the car. I looked at the front, at the spots and headlights, new and glossy, and the cruel absence where the little light should have been in the middle of that ridiculous radiator, the little cream light with 'Wolseley' written in curly red lettering. When my mum had smashed the front of Dad's Wolseley, she had broken every light but that one. I remember being enormously relieved.

'Something wrong?' The son was looking bored. Dad's old passion, now an inconvenience. Three grand.

'Nothing,' I said. 'Thanks for letting me see it.'

'Two and a half.'

'Pardon?'

'Two and a half grand. Go on, it's a bargain. Spent a grand on the engine alone. I'll throw in a new battery. Need the space. We're selling the house, you see. Mam's going to a sheltered. Best thing. Two grand.'

'No,' I said, 'I don't think so. It's not quite what I'm looking for.'

And it wasn't. You can't buy your past back. Not even at the bargain price of two grand. Though I've always wondered if I might have been able to get it for fifteen hundred.

Childhood, eh? Always wondering if you could have got a better deal.

That Wolseley radiator grille haunts me for another reason. It was a dealer in death, a deliverer of premature demise, a provider of . . . soup.

One Saturday, Dad came home with my Uncle John, my mum's younger brother and a great favourite in the house, after a spin up into the Trossachs in the Wolseley. I was playing in the backyard of our Glasgow house, the bottom floor of which was mostly a blood-soaked, gas-on-Tuesdays dental surgery full of moans, screams and terror. The rest of it was fine, though. Don't worry for a moment about my childhood surroundings or upbringing. It was all extremely religious and dental, but on the whole very loving, comfortable and essentially motorised. There was a lot of tooth-brushing and praying, but there are worse things.

Anyway, I clattered round the corner into the driveway to find my uncle and father picking bits of something out of the Wolseley's front end. A large lump of brownness lay on the concrete.

'Come and look at this, Tommy,' shouted John (he was a real uncle, but too young to be taken seriously). 'We've killed a pheasant!'

I had no idea what a pheasant was. Later in my young life I would have trouble knowing the difference between 'peasant' and 'pheasant', for a long time uncertain whether revolting peasants were the same thing as the revolting pheasant the Wolseley had slammed into on the road from Callander. Revolting it certainly was.

Food for me was packaged and came on plates. I may have had some vague notion that beef came from cows, but the actual process of getting it from a large mooing thing to a steaming, gravy-laden Sunday joint was a happy mystery. But pheasants? A chicken was exotic in our house. Years later, I got to know someone from the Shetland island of Unst who told me that until the age of twelve he had assumed that all bananas were black. That's the colour they were when they reached the Baltasound Stores. For us, fruit extended to apples and oranges in season, tangerines at Christmas and strawberries once a year on my sister's July birthday. A melon was a strange, possibly poisonous thing, and mushrooms were regarded with suspicion. My parents came from an industrial working-class background and their voyage into the world of middle-class prosperity brought many changes, many of them dietary. But in the early '60s, the holidays abroad, the arrival of kiwi fruit, the idea that tomatoes might one day be sun-dried . . . all that was in the far, far distant future.

Anyway, the appearance of food in the raw was seen by my mother as a challenge. The pheasant, or what was left of it, was hung in the coal cellar for several weeks, as Mrs Beeton dictated it should. I would sneak down into those dank depths to examine its carcass occasionally, the first dead thing I had ever seen. It was to be an exciting year: within a couple of months I would see my first killing. Of a mackerel, pulled aboard a Carradale fishing boat. I remained unmoved. The pheasant was much more impressive, even if I hadn't seen its actual demise.

At length, the roadkill game was deemed edible, and Mum proceeded to make soup which resonates pungently down the years to my tastebuds. It was like savoury petrol. Nobody liked it. The meat itself had a powerful odour which to my junior nasal passages was reminiscent of the hours I spent with my head poked underneath the carpet and underfelt in the front room, pretending to be a cave explorer, or in a Freudian sense, desperately trying to regain the womb. But the pheasant didn't smell like wombs. It smelt like pre-Dyson floors.

Afterwards, everyone was sick. I've never felt happy since about eating roadkill, though hundreds of rabbits, hares and hedgehogs, not to mention the occasional sheep and indeed pheasant, have fallen victim to my rushing bumpers since. Not even the hedgehogs have tempted me, though I did make an exception when the late Captain Stephen Anderson, soldier, farmer and gospel preacher, ran down a young deer in his Volkswagen Passat estate. It was one of the first Passats, the long, sleek, sculpted ones that looked like cut-price Audis. Pretty much like the relationship between Passats and Audis nowadays, except that the generic Audissat shape is now purest jelly mould. I prefer sleek and sculpted myself.

I was staying in Stephen's wonderful house, Alltnacriche, near Aviemore, in stunningly beautiful alpine conditions, when the Captain of the House arrived back from a trip to Glasgow with a deer strapped to the bonnet, à la Robert De Niro in *The Deer Hunter*. A small deer, virtually a baby, it had been driven down to the A9 by the viciously cold weather. Stephen's Passat had unavoidably clipped it as it scampered about in the inside lane.

Being an experienced deerstalker, grollicker (think guts) and general outdoors type, the Captain expertly put the twitching deerette out of its misery before hoisting it onto the Passat's hood and heading home. I wandered, with the other house guests, out to the garage to examine the trophy, only to find it hanging with its throat cut, blood dripping into a bucket. In the icy chill of that ferociously cold February, it was stiff as a board and the blood was syrupy.

It should have been left to hang for several weeks, but against the Captain's better judgement we ate it two days later. It was like trying to munch lorry tyres, only less tasty.

Since then, I've avoided the consumption of animals which met their end on the dual and single carriageways of our land, or indeed anyone else's land. I have hunted and killed rabbit and hare, shot and butchered my own pigs, cows and sheep, but there's something about roadkill which, if you know its provenance, will inevitably leave you thinking of shattered spotlights, exhaust fumes and unleaded sauce.

Sometimes, in posh restaurants, you catch a whiff of heavy trucks in traffic jams, and wonder about the origins of, say, the dog à l'orange before you. At least I do. Sorry, did I say dog? I meant duck.

Cars were the icons of my childhood, substitutes for the religious symbols that our brand of fundamentalist belief did not permit. There were the Dinkies and Corgis, all now lost in reality but glistening and gleaming, mint and boxed in my mind. By the time they passed from my life, they were tyreless and battered, heaped in old cardboard boxes in lofts which were like miniature scrapyards. First, and most glorious, a present from my mysterious and rarely seen Uncle Jimmy and Aunt Mary, was a long black Cadillac, finned and reeking of an American glamour I had at the age of five not yet seen on television (we didn't have one) or movies (they were the haunt of the Devil, and if Jesus returned to Take You To His Side, he would not be happy to find you in a fleapit).

I can feel that Cadillac's weight in my hands yet. It was a Corgi, of course. They were chunky and glossy, with proper windows and interiors. In comparison to the bare and basic Dinky Toys, the Cadillac was superb. It had suspension, which I quickly broke by pressing too hard on the car as I vroomed it across the knee-skinning roughness of the hessian kitchen floor. Then, when my sister was born, and Mum came back from hospital, she brought a compensatory present for me. Another Corgi car, bought, like my sister, from a shop in Victoria Road called Babyland. It was a Mini. Pale blue, with suspension and a detailed interior but oh, it was so, so small.

'It's awful wee,' I wailed, and not about the newly delivered female child, in whom I had not the slightest interest. And my mother burst into tears.

Later, I was left alone with the sleeping infant in her carry-cot, and I took the opportunity to pick up the Mini and give baby Shiona a sound bludgeoning with it. Fortunately I was not too strong, and the Corgi suspension saved her from much damage other than tyre marks. And parental intervention (which included, as I recall, a good cuffing for me) occurred very shortly after her screaming began.

You'll be pleased to know that we both recovered, and Shiona became Tonto to my Lone Ranger for a brief childhood period, though I did have a tendency to lock her in the coal bunker. These days, she lives a good seven hundred miles away from me, and we are on cordial terms. She drives a Renault Megane Scenic. Sometimes I think everyone with children does.

The toy cars came thick and fast. There were even family heirlooms, like my Uncle John's 1950s Dinky Alfa Grand Prix car, gloriously red, but later scraped and spray-painted metallic blue with some of the touch-up paint from Dad's Ford Zodiac. But most thrilling of all was the arrival, when I was ten, of a Scalextric set.

Dads were always involved, big time, in Scalextric purchases and of course erection, or, if you will, setting up. Because young fingers, for one thing, were not capable of dealing with those impossibly stiff pieces of plastic track, those vicious, skin-trapping locking catches. But, oh, the excitement of preparation for the supposed recipient of the gift, as father and uncles, not to mention any stray male adults, would huddle over the track, the transformer, the controllers, connecting and caressing. For there is a Scalextric-shaped hole in every male human.

The cars in a basic Scalextric set, though, are always disappointing, badly made and designed Minis or boring generic Grand Prix single-seaters. Mine were worse, actually. Motorcycle combinations. Little did I know how crucial the motorbike was to prove in my future professional and personal life. How a sidecar would prove essential to my drinking career. The motorcycle epiphany was just around the corner, but had not yet arrived.

Still, once the basic oval track was set up, the electricity connected and the smell of fizzing 12-volt-infested metal and burning coils filled the air, I was in some kind of weird, hypnotised heaven. The plastic controllers, the old ones that fitted right into your hand, grew hotter and hotter and smoke would occasionally come off the little plastic racing bikes if you over-revved the motors. And then I grew bored; basically because my dad and John hogged the thing for hours at a time. They were Stirling Moss and Fangio, or they would have been if Santa had not delivered a motorcycle combination Isle of Man TT version of Scalextric. Instead they were . . . well. Even if motorcyclists like John Surtees and Mike Hailwood, and latterly the likes of Barry Sheene and Carl Fogerty are household names, who knows anything about sidecar racers? On Boxing Day, Dad went out and bought a BRM and a Vanwall, plastic version thereof, from the Clyde Model Dockyard, home from home for staring-eyed children and their parents, as well as solitary adult males with suspicious tastes in Hornby Dublo.

I grew bored with the cars, too. And though as the years passed that Scalextric outfit was enlarged, laid out in the loft on plywood, added to again and again, it gradually faded from my interest and memory until Mum gave the whole lot to a jumble sale. I was, of course, furious, despite having left home for university by then. Suddenly, the smell of overstressed electrical circuits, the humming whine of the cars, came back to me, and I longed for those mesmerised hours spent watching little bits of plastic whizzing around a track and, more often than not, spinning off. By that time, though, I had a real car, and real girls to pursue, and the anger passed. Scalextric was forgotten.

Of course, once you have children of your own, that Scalextric-shaped absence in the heart begins to tingle, and you start to propagandise on the product's behalf, whispering in your bairns' ears that, hey, maybe they'd fancy an outfit for Christmas. Michael Schumacher's Let's Piss Off David Coulthard Maximum Thrill German Grand Prix set, perhaps.

But I'm not that kind of person. I'm not that sad dad, that imposer of my tastes on my kids. Well, actually I am, but much, much sadder. After I'd bought Magnus and James the Rally 400 Scalextric set-up and they had trashed the cars within a week by stamping on them, I removed the whole thing to my office, bought four new vehicles (Mitsubishi Lancer, Subaru WRX, and, umm, two motoryycle-and-sidecar combinations), some extra track and a lap counter, and set up an enormous, if rather peculiar, semi-square layout around and over my computers and fax machines. The office (in a barn next to the house) is now a place I can repair to with a bottle of Laphroaig and, perhaps with a pal, engage in drunken driving on a 1:32 scale. Children are not permitted.

Pathetic? I know, I know. But it's better than owning something disgraceful like a Ford Escort/RS Turbo with extra plastic skirts and an imitation penis front spoiler thing. Which I did, albeit briefly. Buying tyres at £130 a time soon lost its appeal.

Perhaps the fact that my first Scalextric layout came equipped with motorcycle combinations instead of cars was the first step on the road to two-wheeled perdition I still find myself on. For here's the awful truth: as well as having lived a life mapped out in car ownership, I have also, for four decades, been obsessed with motorcycles, off and on. And sometimes, when trying to stay on some diseased, unroadworthy moped or unwieldy superbike, I have failed and been off when I should have been on, and painfully at that.

It's not as if we were a motorcycling family. It was four wheels all the way, be it my dad's weekly perusal of *Motor* and *Autocar*, or the annual trek to Glasgow's Kelvin Hall for the Scottish Motor Show. My first self-propelled, as in able to walk, visit there is etched in my memory because it was the occasion of my first encounter with the forces of law and order, in all their intimidating magnificence. As my father gazed longingly at the Vauxhall stand – and I remember this precisely because he ended up buying a Vauxhall – I was filled with a burning desire to go back and look at the packed Jaguar display, where there were queues of snotty six-year-olds like myself, all waiting to smear their nasal secretions over the red leather seats of a glistening Jaguar Mark Two. Boy-children (girls? What use were they?) used to throng the motor show, all lugging piles of glossy brochures which they could later use for bedroom-festooning. I never had the nerve to demand, say, an Aston Martin brochure, as I was more than aware that, in reality, I was not a prospective purchaser. At six, I had a sense of propriety about these things.

Be that as it may, off I went to find the Jags, and became hopelessly, tinily lost in the seething mass of motor-mad humanity, a humanity so large that the sense of constricting panicky lostness is with me now, all six-and-a-bit foot of me. You are never so horribly lost as when your vision is restricted to a moving forest of trousered thighs. In any city other than stunted Glasgow, it would have been knees.

I began to roar and howl, as is always advised in such circumstances. Soon I was gazing not at trousered thighs, but at two pairs of dark-blue serge-clad knees. Tilting my head upwards I saw, seemingly miles up in the air, and way beyond mountainous expanses of glittering buttons and uniform blue-black, two ruddy and terrifying faces, each surmounted by flat peaked caps bearing chequered bands. Policemen. I had heard of such beings, had glimpsed them in the street, but had never expected to have any dealings with them in person.

One crouched down to something approximating my level, like a giant redwood suddenly collapsing in on itself. 'Now, now, sonny,' he said, softly guttural, one gigantically heavy hand resting on my shoulder, 'Are you lost?' What a stupid question. And a worrying one, in my circumstances. I was clearly going to be arrested, and would never see my parents again. Also, Dad would get into trouble with Mum, I was certain, if he arrived home without me.

'Yes, I was lost,' I hiccuped, sighed and sobbed.

'And what's your name? Are you here with your daddy?'

'T . . . Tommy Morton,' I replied, adding in the smartass way that was to serve me ill throughout my future career, 'and I'm not with my daddy. I'm lost.'

I was whisked off to a hidden office which smelt of disinfectant, and handed a free paper cup of Irn Bru, which Dad had earlier been unable to obtain for me because, he had claimed, of the queues. A tinny Tannoy announcement quickly fetched my bereft father, who found me swapping tales of the comparative merits of Dinkies and Corgis with the two unhatted polis, whose names were Frank and Billy. I was expecting a cuff round the ear, but instead I was asked, very nicely I thought, not to tell my mother that I had been lost. Of course I wouldn't; of course not.

'Mum!' I shouted, when at length we were reunited with my shopping female parent at the George Cross end of Great Western Road. 'Guess what! Dad lost me!' The look of awesome fury on my mother's face was quickly transmuted into a conversation with my father which, though necessarily muted by the crowds thronging the public pavement we were on, clearly carried enormous punishing force as far as Dad was concerned. Then I saw something strange.

It was behind a massive plate-glass window, and it was a motorbike. I knew about motorbikes, had seen and heard their smoky puttering, felt a vague queasy nervousness at the sight of roaring, helmeted, black-leather-clad men on machines which made my mum and dad wince. But I had never seen anything like this.

For a start, it was absolutely vast, and utterly black. It was the personification of mechanical evil, and it reeked of death and danger. If I had been older, I would have recognised that it also exuded a sexuality of the most brutal kind. 'Dad,' I said, interrupting the whispered harangue he was suffering from my mother, 'what's this?'

Relieved at the distraction, he came over to the window, which belonged to a motorcycle showroom, still there, called Victor Devine. Unlike me, he could read the typewritten label taped to the floor in front of this monstrous piece of engineering. Standing still, it seemed like some kind of chained beast, maddened and sullen, looking for a chance to pounce.

'It's a Brough Superior,' he said. And even the words sounded hard, risky, potent. Bruff. Super. Eeyore.

It came from a place far beyond my ken, that bike. I couldn't even envisage riding such a complicated, raw lump of metal. But, for years afterwards, when I thought of motorcycles, I thought of black. I thought of something hugely dangerous (partly because Mum dragged us both away from the window, muttering, 'Motorbikes are deathtraps,' a litany I was to hear repeated many, many times). I thought of oiliness and bigness and ferocious, obvious power. I certainly did not think of a Honda 50, the first motorbike I was ever to ride on the open road.

There has never been a motorcycle so wrapped in doom-laden symbolism as the Brough Superior. The Vincent Black Shadows and Lightnings probably have more mystique and were better, faster bikes. The Brough was a bitsa, a vastly expensive one, designed and built by one George Brough from the best components he could find, to produce what was called in the 1920s and '30s 'the Rolls-Royce of motorcycles'. Enthusiasts still jabber on about the Brough Superior SS100 Alpine Grand Sport's 1000cc V-twin JAP engine, Bonniksen speedometer, Brooks saddle, Sturmey Archer gearbox, Pilgrim oil pump and Castle leading-link front forks. They dribble. They lust.

Thirty years after that machine was made, as I gazed in that shop window, I was conscious not of it looking old, but of its fearful, awe-inspiring appearance. And I had never even heard of Lawrence of Arabia.

It was as if the bike carried with it all the strangeness and tragedy of T.E. Lawrence's death, and somehow communicated that to a six-year-old boy. I have no idea if that machine had any connection with Lawrence. Nowadays, any SS100 will have some spurious Lawrence anecdote attached, and consequently an inflated price tag. The actual bike he died on is owned by somebody called John Weekly who, I heard lately, was asking a million quid for it. But because Lawrence either owned or had on long-term loan no fewer than seven of these massive, dangerous (very badly underbraked, a bit like some modern Harleys) playthings, you can see how the dealers might have a field day.

Lawrence of Arabia, though. Think Peter O'Toole in the eponymous film. Not the one called *Peter O'Toole*, the one called *Lawrence of Arabia*. Imagine a hero so heroic that he out-heroed Biggles, the Duke of Wellington, Ayrton Senna and Mother Teresa of Calcutta, not to mention, say, Muhammad Ali, all put together. And that he was as handsome as Sting before he went bald, as clever as a supercomputer, and wrote better than Irvine Welsh (or at least wasn't so forthright as Irv would have been about being buggered by an Arab). Thomas Edward Lawrence was all that and more in the 1920s and '30s.

But the being-buggered-by-an-Arab thing, which no doubt reminded him of public school's anal delights, and the coy description of which is still excised from some copies of *Seven Pillars of Wisdom*, left the highly strung Lawrence in a bit of a state vis-à-vis gender issues. And so the whole weird and sad business of enlisting in the RAF as an ordinary airman arose, as if Mike Tyson had suddenly tried to enlist in the Boy Scouts, only with homoerotic overtones and a bit of erudite quoting from the original Greek.

I do not propose to go into the relationship between subliminal sexual urges and motorcycles at this point, but it is a fact that Lawrence was completely bonkers when it came to bikes. He named each of his seven – that perfect number – Broughs 'Boanerges' I to VII as in James and John the sons of Zebedee, disciples of Christ, who were nicknamed by their master 'Boanerges, which is, Sons of Thunder' (Gospel according to St Mark, ch. 3, v. 17). Between 1922 and 1935 he covered no fewer than 299,000 miles on these fire-spitting creatures. Of course, Boanerges VII – registration GW 2275 – killed him, not due to excess speed, a thrill which the camel-galloping ex-terrorist leader loved, but due to the Brough's instability and poor brakes. The SS100 was capable of 108 mph, but when Lawrence crested that Dorset hill on 13 May 1935, he was doing only about 40. Confronted with two boys wobbling about on overloaded delivery pushbikes, he braked, swerved and crashed at about 20 mph. He wasn't wearing a helmet, and fractured his skull. He died six days later in hospital.

The curious outcome of Lawrence's untimely demise (apart from all the nonsense about a plot to murder him, the mysterious flowers still left at the scene of the accident on the anniversary of his death, and the quasi-religious cult which surrounds the man) was the introduction in 1973 of a law making it compulsory for motorcyclists to wear crash helmets.

That was the result of a campaign started by one Hugh Cairns, the neurosurgeon who had operated on Lawrence and who was so dismayed by the extent of the war hero's injuries from such a slow-speed crash that he battled for the rest of his life to achieve cranial protection for bikers. Despite his best efforts, even today most motorcycling fatalities are caused by accidents at less than 30 mph.

The sight of that Brough in the shop window implanted a paradigm in my mind of what a motorbike should look like. Years later, backstage in Hollywood at *The Tonight Show*, I met the host Jay Leno. He came rampaging up to me, bellowing in a truly awful Scottish accent: 'Och aye the noo, where's yon fine Scotch laddie, hoots mon!' His mother came from Greenock, where I presume people must speak like that. After some general conversation ('So, how's that Billy Connolly? Next time you see him back in Scawtland, you tell him Jay was asking for him!') I began asking him about his bike and car collection, one of the finest private collections in the USA, and a great source of rivalry between Leno and his sort-of-buddy Jerry Seinfeld, who's also a wheelnut.

'Yeah, I've got a Vincent Black Shadow. Sometimes I ride it around LA too. What's the point of a bike you don't ride? It's British bikes I like. I like a bike you can look through.'

A bike you can look through. What he meant was a motorbike with all its gubbins exposed, so you can see its guts, and through the engine to the other side. In other words, not one of those plastic training-shoe motorbikes, all fairing and cowling, which are the essence of modern sports bike design.

You can just about see through a Brough Superior, though its enormous JAP engine is crammed into the frame like an elephant in a packing case. I have seen several restored examples since that childhood encounter with the battered, oily monster in Victor Devine's window. It had a torn single saddle, I remember, big enough to handle a horse's arse.

All of the Broughs retain that sense of sullen power, of sheer, brutal, in-your-face exultation in speed. And they reek of death. I knew that, somehow, long before I had even heard of T.E. Lawrence. But then that is the point of motorbikes. Death and the thrill of its avoidance. They are the un-Volvos.

I had a car and a bike when I was seven, just before we moved from the wicked city streets of Glasgow to the seaside delights of Troon in Ayrshire. Each was used to make unauthorised trips to the nearest newsagent's, clutching sufficient cash to buy a *Beano* on one occasion and a *Dandy* on the other. It was only about 140 metres to the shop, along the pavement by busy Pollokshaws Road on Glasgow's south side. Each time, I made it to the shop successfully. Each time, I peed my pants in the excitement of disobedience, driving the little Tri-ang pedal car and the Speedmaster Raleigh balloon-tyred bike (with stabilisers) all that way without telling my mother.

I still get excited when heading off on a long journey by bike or car, but that early incontinence has more or less been conquered through being clipped round the ear on both of those rather damp early voyages of discovery and comic-buying.

Just five years ago I went out for a drink with the editor of the *Dandy* and told him this story. He proceeded to buy me so much alcohol that I came closer than I ever have to repeating the pant-wetting incident, doubtless for his eternal anecdotal benefit. Instead, next morning, I breakfasted on unflushed toilet and had to do the radio show I was then employed by the BBC to perpetrate on Scotland in a horizontal position, with a bucket by my head for occasional vomiting.

I should add a short message to Messrs Aston and Martin, who in July 1999 kindly lent me one of only two DB7 Vantages then available as test cars in the UK. Driving that leather-lined beast, all creaky walnut and half-tamed British Bulldog speed, from Edinburgh to Fife was a wonderful, GATSO-camera usurping experience. Never before have I been saluted by the toll collectors on the Forth Road Bridge. Thank you, Mr Aston, Mr Martin. And, in view of the foregoing remarks concerning the peeing of pants, I would add that the stains on the driver's seat were not urine, nor any other embarrassing human secretion. They were coffee. Well, coffee and Halfords own-brand upholstery cleaner, which I admit may have been a mistake on hand-cut Connolly hide. But I was embarrassed. Anyway, it wasn't pee. I want to make that clear. No matter what the position of the stain might have made you think.

Just fit some bloody cupholders.

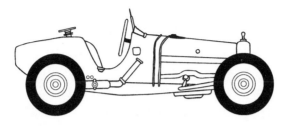

DESCRIBING 105 MAKES WITH 270 HALF-TONE PHOTOGRAPHS AND NUMEROUS LINE DRAWINGS

*T*he *Observer's Book of Automobiles* both soothed and fuelled my childhood obsession with cars; for my nine-year-old son James Patrick (JP), its digital equivalent is a Sony Playstation game called Gran Turismo II.

Gran Turismo is not just a racing game. You have to choose the car you want to race, its tyres, tyre pressure, suspension settings and, for all I know, colour of upholstery, and you can tune it to within an inch of its life. It is breathtakingly – some (I for one) would say tediously – accurate. Yet it has given JP a fascination for real cars not shared by his older brother and unforeseen by his father who, thanks to *The Observer's Book of Automobiles*, lived through the same phase of existence. And, to an extent, is still doing so.

'Look at that! A Mercedes SLK! Have you driven one, Dad?' To which the answer, thanks to my rather embarrassing second-string career in the world of motoring telly, is yes. And son, it's a ridiculously expensive piece of nonsense for rich poseurs who like to reek of quality as well as wealth.

'Dad! Dad! A Citroën Saxo! You *hate* them, don't you!'

Yes, son, it is, and I do. In fact, I hate all Citroëns, especially the 2CV, that sardine tin upside-down pram now being romantically rediscovered by people with neither aesthetic sense nor mechanical insight. Citroëns are, in fact, evil. It is not that they are French. Peugeots are French, and are even made by the same company as Citroëns. But they're quite boringly good, whereas Citroëns are prime examples of suppurating moral depravity on four wheels. I will explain, but not yet.

Any journey is for JP a ferment of discovery. He is thrilled by Hyundais, Audi TTs, Jaguars and especially, for some reason, by Minis. He loves Minis. As I write, BMW is hanging onto the new Mini and the old Mini is to die, and not before time. Its design is so far beyond its sell-by date that it really ought to have been killed off years ago.

Sentimentality? No. Not even for the brilliant door-handle receptacles designed, it is said, so that Sir Alec Issigonis could store a bottle of his favourite whisky in one without it rolling about. At least it was an improvement on Issigonis's previous effort, the Morris Minor, which allowed bottles to fly everywhere.

JP is mad about cars. He has begun, at his own instigation, I hasten to add, buying die-cast models and his enjoyment of their design details is a pleasure to watch. His latest acquisition is a Spanish one-24th version of something called the Chrysler Atlantic, which looks like a cross between a Morgan, an XK Jaguar and the Batmobile. It is uncannily ugly and seductively curvy at the same time. Occasionally I find JP looking at it in a kind of awed wonder.

'Dad, this car's got a face! Look at it . . . that's the eyes, the headlights. The two bits in the middle are the nose, and the bumper's the mouth.'

Yep. That's how it was, how it is, how it ought to be. But most modern cars don't have faces, JP.

'I know. What's the hardest car to recognise?'

Hmm . . . tricky one. Loads of cars just look the same, JP, don't they?

'Honda S2000, Dad. All those cars with no roofs make it look like nothing.' And of course, he's right. I just hadn't thought of it that way before.

Have I driven a Chrysler Atlantic, he demands? Nope. But sometimes, when he's at school, I pick up the toy's carefully preserved cardboard box

(Tuitotoy, Originales Miniatures) and open the nicely engineered doors, turn the steering wheel and watch the thick plastic wheels tilt round; I spin the back ones, with their hollow, sightly cheap rattle; I look at it from every angle and just enjoy its existence. And wish, and half-dream of ownership and driving. As you do, even with a Land Rover and iron mental discipline. As JP does.

For me, it was the Lamborghini P400 Miura as featured in *The Observer's Book of Automobiles*, say the 1967 edition, one of the last of the great original L.A. Manwaring-edited books, before the Olyslager Organisation took over production and the quaint character of the tiny, pocket-sized hardbacks began to disappear.

The Lamborghini is on page 146. Lancia's gorgeous linear Fulvia coupé, too subtle for a schoolboy, is opposite, but the Lamborghini page is the one that dreams are made of. The prancing bull logo, even the name of the firm, Automobili Feruccio Lamborghini SAS, with the address in Bologna, Italy.

The picture: slightly coarse-screened, but communicating a beauty so extreme, so perfect, that it still takes the breath away. This was the shape which adorned hundreds of pages of schoolbooks, which still springs to the nib if a car-doodling moment approaches. Low, sleek, phallic before I had even heard of the word, but beyond all feline, feminine, brutal and just the car, *The Car*, in its entirety. Forget practicality, passengers, rough terrain . . . ignore everything but speed, power and beauty. The Lamborghini P400 Miura Sports Coupé. Even now, it makes me want to cry.

Then the statistics: number of cylinders, 'V12 transverse, rear-mounted' (actually, mid-mounted, but let's not split crankcases over that); 'cubic capacity 3929cc. Brake horse power 350 (430 Sprint)'. Holy smoke! What's this? There's a Sprint option! What can that be like? All is revealed in the next few words, the longed-for words which do not always appear in L.A. Manwaring's spec. listings: 'Max. mph 186 or 200'. *Two hundred!* It is the fastest thing in the book, the fastest car in the world then, outside of a race-bred mudguardless monstrosity, and it looks . . . it

INTERNAL COMBUSTION

looks . . . it looks like there is, can be, nothing else. Ever.

Then there's Manwaring's actual description, hilariously inadequate in its sobriety: 'Low, sleek and sporting . . . flowing wing-line to flat tail panel, the lower portion of which consists of air-outlet grille large oblong tail lamps.'

None of that matters. You know, just from that tiny, two-and-a-half by one inch picture, that this is the design by which all your standards will be set forever. It is still the case. Show me a Lotus Elise. Oh, do piss off. Here, turn to page 146. Look and slobber. What about the new Diablo? Sorry, not even Lamborghini can equal page 146's 1960s work of genius. I have been in a Diablo. I didn't drive it, but the owner, David Jones, did take me for a trip across the Tay Bridge. It was like being in an incredibly noisy and very uncomfortable shoe. Lined completely with purple suede, it sounded like a Shackleton at full take-off speed and went like a Tornado jet. It also, in my humble opinion, looked like it had been made out of old cornflakes packets and sprayed with Humbrol enamel. But what can I say? You grow up, the real thing comes along. And it's shite. Well, not shite, but purple and plasticky. I mean, you'd take one if somebody offered it to you, but you wouldn't go out and buy one yourself. Even if you had the money. Which, of course, I don't. And I have a Land Rover, which is the anti-Lamborghini. Maybe that's why I like it so much. As a colleague once said, cycling out of a BBC car park, puffing at a fag, when I yelled a good-natured insult at him about healthy smoking: 'Bit o' yin, Tom, bit o' yang.' Quite.

The Observer's Book of Automobiles was first published in 1955, the year I was born, and every edition of the series is now, to a greater or lesser extent, a collector's item. Like those 'buy a newspaper from your birth date' offers, grown men – some women, but mostly men – can seek out *The Observer's Book of Automobiles* from a particular year, and transport themselves back to the ease and comfort of childhood, to the innocence of automotive dreams. For me it's 1967.

I was eleven (going on twelve – my birthday's in December) and at my peak of passion and yearning for cars. They represented a longed-for adulthood, and an astonishing world of glamour, speed and mechanical brilliance. This was the real world reference for the stuff I tried to build from Lego and Meccano, existing somewhere out there, shrunk to tiny black-and-white pictures on a page. Could something like the Checker Aerobus A-12W8M limousine actually exist, all nineteen feet seven-and-a-quarter inches of it, with its nine doors and capacity for twelve passengers? In that alien parallel universe called America, it could indeed.

Would I ever see a car called an Acadian? Would I ever go to its homeland, Canada? And what about a Zil ('very large, heavy-looking car') from Russia, or an OSCA from Italy ('unusual combination of flowing curves and razor-edged styling')? And where are they now? In museums, certainly, with the factories that made them converted to other uses like the assembly of Taiwanese computer components. Either that or razed to the ground.

Elsewhere, there are eerie premonitions of what was to come in my own life: an MG 1100 saloon, which would be my first car; the Singer Chamois my mother would acquire in 1969; the Vauxhall Cresta Dad would buy in 1968; the beloved Wolseley 6/110.

Flower Power, the Summer of Love, Jefferson Airplane, Moby Grape, LSD, Haight Ashbury and the beginnings of Pink Floyd. For me it was all Triumph 2000s and Morgans, Masarati Sebring GTI coupés, the gorgeous (but not quite as gorgeous as the Miura) Iso Grifo GL coupé.

The year 1967 was a watershed for motoring, and indeed for *The Observer's Book of Automobiles*. It was the year Japan entered the lists, big time. Even Stirling Moss's gloriously peculiar introduction deals with the advent of vehicles from the Land of the Rising Sun, a mere twenty-two years after Hiroshima:

> Since the last edition of this book appeared, the new international formula for Grand Prix racing cars has come into force . . . the coming season promises to be a very exciting one, with new cars and engines . . .
>
> My appeal for road safety is, as usual, especially to young

readers and I would remind them to LOOK RIGHT, LOOK LEFT and LOOK RIGHT AGAIN before crossing the road.

When I was a boy, this book was a huge comfort, soothing me in the terrors of the night; I am not ashamed to admit that it did so long into my teens. If I woke to the sound of some huge industrial plant thumping far away in the dark distance – it took me years to realise I was listening to my own heartbeat – I would slowly leaf through one or other of my various worn copies, settling on curiosities like the Mini Scorpion Saloon, or one of my obscure favourites, the beautifully curvy Saab Sonnet II Sports coupé. Doubtless the obsession with curves was a precursor of sexual awakening, though I gained as much reassurance in the watches of the night from the severe lines of the Mercedes 230 SL or the BMW 2000 coupé. No Freudian analysis necessary.

I wonder what the British manufacturers of such utterly outmoded models as the Sunbeam Rapier and Rover Three Litre made of the way such names as Mazda, Toyota – with the Corolla De Luxe Saloon and the astonishing (and very, very curvy) 2000 GT coupé – Daihatsu and Honda suddenly popped up. And if you compared the 2000 GT with, say, the Morris Minor, surely the writing was on the wall for the old timers of the British car industry. In fact, only TVR and Morgan survive from 1967 as truly independent companies.

The entry on Rover is one of the biggest in the book, and how poignant it is to read of J.K. Starley and W. Sutton founding the company in 1877, building penny-farthing bicycles in Coventry. The first Rover motorcycle came out in 1903, and the first car the following year. Between 1950 and 1961, Manwaring writes, the firm pioneered gas-turbine cars, a technology only now being seriously re-examined.

But the gas-turbine prototypes are broken-up or museum pieces, and now Rover is being broken-up, its final owners, the great rival BMW, hanging on, for the moment, only to the post-modern Mini replacement, and letting the rest go to an uncertain fate with the apparently well-meaning Phoenix Consortium. No comfort there for the workers of the

West Midlands. And a queasy feeling when, restless at 3 a.m., I pick up this tiny blue book and look for something to quiet a racing mind.

I usually find it, though. You always get a laugh out of a Wartburg or Zaporogets (Komunard Factory, Zaporozh, USSR, the predecessor of the later Lada–Fiat collaboration in the guise of a distended Fiat 600). Or a Vauxhall, for that matter. You can bore yourself to sleep with the endless pages about number plates of the world, or grin at the picture of the Chrysler Turboflite when the caption asks, 'Is this the shape of things to come?' Or relax into the sheer stupid beauty of the Fiat Abarth 1000 SP Spider ('low sporting lines').

You're probably thinking, this sad git has kept that *Observer's Book of Automobiles* for thirty-three years, hugging it to him when he ought to have been out experiencing the world, screwing, taking drugs, drinking and reading Wilbur Smith novels. Would that it had been so! The truth is that, like thousands of other sad and nostalgic middle-aged men, I had to seek out my 1967 lump of memories using the online service provider Bookfinder.com. I quickly discovered that pre-1970 books are expensive and difficult to track down. One bookseller told me that they move faster than almost anything else he stocks, because once a man of a certain age picks one up at a sale, he just has to have it.

Eventually I tracked down a copy of the 1967 book I had long ago lost, laid aside, exchanged for sex, whatever. It was in a Helensburgh shop which operates only by mail and the net. The owner doesn't even like speaking to you on the phone, preferring to deal exclusively by e-mail. It cost me £12 plus postage, for an edition with its dustjacket worn but intact – a bit faded but complete and readable. And it's a delight. Better than librium, marijuana or indeed gin and tonic, depending on the circumstances. And the combinations employed.

Just after I'd acquired it, my father told me he still had a 1972 edition, one he'd bought for himself when I was fifteen and obsessed with motorbikes. I have it before me. It is in immaculate condition, but while the 1967 version has a daft cover-drawing at least attempting to communicate some of the joy of motoring, the 1972 edition has . . . wait for it . . . two Morris Marinas on the cover. A car so boring that it has never attained, and never will attain, classic or collectable status, unless among the mentally ill and downright perverse. There can be nothing kitsch about a Marina. It is, to use a Scottish word, not kitsch, just keech. Purest jobbie, if you prefer.

And that picture sets the tone for the 1972 *Observer's Book of Automobiles*. L.A. Manwaring has gone, along with all the historical details, the bonkers introduction by Stirling Moss, the eccentric descriptions, the amazing list of number plate codes and international identification marks. Instead, there is a cursory set of specifications 'compiled by the well-known Olyslager Organisation', but missing out the glories of the Zil and Zaporogets, and even Abarth. Wartburg is still there, though the Knight looks almost normal, as long as you don't read the engine details and find out that it's a two-stroke.

It's a characterless book, printed web-offset for the first time on cheap paper, though there are still some nutty vehicles hidden away among the tedium of the Ford Escort 1300 XL and the Daf 44 Estate Car. There is the misconceived but wonderfully daft VW-Porsche, the epically curvy Marcos Three Litre, the Lotus Europa twin-cam and the completely manic Citroën SM, which may have stood for sado-masochism but probably didn't in 1972, when such habits did not exist. Except, maybe, in France. But daftest of all is the Technical Exponents TX Tripper, a kind of stretched beach buggy with a Triumph engine, 'formerly known as Fairthorpe'. It's the only really crazy car in the entire publication.

There are several vehicles, though, which I either owned or drove, from the Simca 1100 GLS my mum had to the Mini Clubman Estate I traded in my first wife's Morris 1100 for, a car without suspension or indeed any redeeming qualities whatsoever. Certainly not the fake wood side-stripes. And the Avenger I ended up buying for £300 in 1984, in the throes of marital separation, and which possessed a back seat so shiny that one son slid across it and split his head wide open on the door handle. Safety, eh? I spent a whole childhood without seat belts in all my family's various vehicles, and never got scratched. And yet the day I pick up my two sons in a 1972 Hillman Avenger, made in Linwood, Renfrewshire, one of them gets injured as I go round an innocent turn. Nostalgia's no good if it's not retrofitted with rear seat belts and child seats.

But there it is, on page sixteen, the Austin/Morris 1800 MKII S; the landcrab, Alex Issigonis's stretched Mini, and the first car I ever drove. I must have been sixteen, a sullen, reluctant member of the family, holidaying in a caravan in the Lake District. And on a quiet perimeter road at the Bassenthwaite caravan site, I cautiously steered Dad's Morris 1800 S at 5 mph, round and round and round, sometimes even getting into second gear. Which, considering the awfulness of the cable-operated gearchange, was pretty damned impressive if you ask me.

'Dad?'

'Yes, JP.'

'What's the fastest car you've ever driven? Is it the Aston Martin DB7 Vantage or the BMW M5? Or the Nissan Skyline?'

'Dunno, JP.'

'Dad?'

'Uh-huh?'

'I'm thinking of buying a Mini for Gran Turismo and tuning it. Do you think that's a good idea?'

'No, son. Well, not really. Why don't you have a look at this *Observer's Book of Automobiles* instead? Read something for a change.'

'Dad, I read cheats and hints for the Playstation all the time. But okay. Hey . . . what's this?'

'That's a Jensen Interceptor. It's an old car from the 1960s. It was dead fast. And that . . . that's a Lamborghini P400 Miura.'

'Dad?'

'Yes! What!'

'Can we get Playstation Two, and Gran Turismo for it?'

'Maybe.'

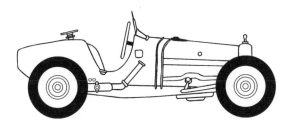

BAD MOTOR SCOOTER

Y ou know Gordon and Gillian's eldest, Peter?'
'Jim's big brother? Yes.'
'Well, he's running about on a motorbike.'
'What? What age is he?'
'Well, it's a moped. I don't know . . . '
'Sixteen. Is it sixteen for a moped? Or seventeen?'
'He's not sixteen. I think he's fifteen. Anyway, he's riding it without a helmet, that's the thing. Or he had this friend on, and he had a helmet, but a bicycle helmet.'
'What, he had a pal riding pillion? On a moped?'
'Anyway, riding along all mad and wobbling and daft, right in the road.'
'Well, Johnny's not going along there if Jim's going to be involved in that in any way, shape or form. Bloody hell! No insurance, no helmets, bet there were no gloves or boots?'
'No.'
'God almighty, I've spent thirty years of my life not falling off motorbikes, not geting hurt on them, and you've spent years falling off them and getting hurt, and I'm damned if my son's going to get crippled on some two-bit unlicensed moped, just because his pal's big brother wants to show off.'

'I stopped.'

'What?'

'I stopped riding bikes after that VW Beetle hit me on Great Western Road and I burst my spleen. I didn't spend years falling off them. I fell off twice. Or I was hit twice by dickhead males in cars.'

'Anyway, I don't mind the boys riding bikes. But if they're going to do it, they'll go for instruction, and learn properly, and have the right gear, and they won't get a sniff of a bike until I think they're safe. Is that fair?'

'Absolutely . . . '

Except it isn't. It's hypocrisy. It's grown-up, parental talk, self-satisfied and post-middle age, comfortable, all scars healed, scared-of-dying stuff.

I'm thinking of a Ford Anglia, resprayed black and gold, owned by the Johnstone twins, renegade co-religionists, mad bastard terrors of the Youth Fellowship at our church. One berserk Sunday, they gave me and two other, more junior, members of the YF a lift from Troon to Prestwick for some kind of evangelical rally, and afterwards Curly Johnstone, his brother Pierce beside him in the front, decided to give us a demonstration of just what his Anglia could do.

Remember the Ford Anglia? Curly's was a Ford Anglia Super, equipped with 48.5 horse power and a 1198cc engine. It had a flick-back roofline and frog-eye front which looked amazingly rakish, outlandish even. Crammed into the back with my pals Stevie and Donnie, I was speechless with awe at being permitted to share such a fantastical motorised space with the dangerous Johnstone brothers. Shoulder to shoulder, silent, rapt at Curly's skill, Stevie, Donnie and I stayed locked as one against the centrifugal force as Curly threw the screeching little car out along Prestwick main street towards the airport, and what was at that time the only stretch of proper dual carriageway in our part of Ayrshire. As the 30 mph limit dropped behind us, Curly wound the little Anglia up to a third-gear scream, and all three of us in the back craned as best we could to see the speedometer. It was jammed solid on its upper limit of eighty.

'Probably nearer ninety,' said Pierce, as the turn-off on the right to Prestwick Airport loomed.

At this time, Prestwick Airport's terminal was an ultra-modern edifice unsurpassed in Scotland. Vast, far too big for the traffic it handled or would ever handle, it was open twenty-five hours a day, and glinted and gleamed in neon and glass, promising almost inconceivable romance. It was Scotland's only transatlantic gateway, and so when we went there, like nervous pilgrims, for a family cafeteria meal (oh the treat! Square sliced sausage Mum didn't have to cook herself!), or an impossibly profligate sandwich with liquid lettuce, ultra late at 10 p.m., we mingled with alien creatures called Americans, and listened to Tannoy announcements calling the faithful to fly to Boston, New York, Los Angeles. Sometimes, on Sundays such as this one, we all sneaked in for an illicit, Sabbath-breaking Coca-Cola. But not tonight. Curly was more keen on demonstrating his capacity to be Jochen Rindt, his favourite Grand Prix driver.

I was maybe thirteen. I was wearing a kilt, I remember that, Ancient Douglas tartan. I had been bought it aged eleven for my favourite uncle John's wedding, and forced to continue wearing it despite suddenly shooting up in height aged twelve and now, spotty and adolescent, considering it the ultimate in naffness. I still had the bejewelled *skean-dhu* in my sock, though, which could have been classed as an offensive weapon, and was useful for flicking the suppurating yellow heads off my plukes. Underneath, for the record, I wore swimming trunks.

Anyway, we came hurtling towards the airport exit, and I thought for a moment that Curly was going to try and swerve at 80 mph, or however fast we were going, across the opposite carriageway and into the car park. Then I saw the motorbike.

Who knows what kind it was? The number plate was white letters on black, and something in me says it looked British. The pillion passenger had no helmet on, I remember that. It was before the change, when the process started by that T.E. Lawrence head injury came to fruition, and helmets became compulsory. A big bike, something substantial. The rider was crouched down low over clip-on bars. A BSA Gold Star perhaps, or a Bonneville.

The snapshot, over Curly and Pierce's shoulders, through the Anglia's smeared windscreen: heading straight for the bike, the pillion passenger's face, frozen in shock, unidentifiable, but pale, topped by a shock of slipstreamed hair. In the headlights, flash-frozen. Sound: a whining, screaming, drumming from the overstretched Anglia motor, and in the background Curly and Pierce laughing, as the bike and the monstrous, distorted face of the passenger, hands formally clasped behind him on a chrome seat bar, as he filled the windscreen . . .

Then we were past. Pierce's voice: 'Made it, bruv. Inches to spare. Bet that gave them a bit of turn, eh?'

I realised several things that night, when I was safely back home in my bed, reliving the nerve-shearing horror of that deliberate near-miss. One was that my sympathies were entirely with the people on the bike. I knew that games like the one Curly had played were insanely dangerous, potentially fatal, and that even the thin sheen of tin provided by a Ford Anglia meant that we had been the bullying aggressor against the vulnerable. Secondly, I determined never to ride pillion on anyone's motorbike. A month or two previously, a sixth-year pupil at my school had crashed his Norton Commando, a present from rich parents, into a concrete post on Welbeck Crescent, next to Troon's municipal golf course. He had broken his back, but his pillion, who was wearing a helmet, had been decapitated, it was quietly whispered, by the fence wire. We would gather in small, schoolbagged groups to stare at the piece of fencing, now repaired, and wonder. Paralysis from the waist down seemed to be preferable. Nowadays I'm not so sure.

Thirdly, I realised that born-again Christianity of the kind adhered to in our little church did not necessarily lead to safe, responsible driving, kindness, goodness or even sanity. All in all, some important lessons were learned that night. I also determined never to wear a kilt again. Those swimming trunks just got too sweaty in a pinch.

Two years after this, I bought my first motorbike. With Stevie, I had begun drooling over *Motorcycle News* and mentally fingering through the unthinkable specifications of Harley Davidsons: 1,000, 2,000cc? That was a car! And so I had to get onto two motorised wheels myself, even if I couldn't ride legally. A motorbike it had to be.

Well, I say motorbike; I mean scooter. It was a Vespa 150, the classic Piaggio, and it had belonged to Dougie Walker, a pal who lived just across the road; he had bought it from the father of a Youth Fellowship acquaintance of mine, a girl called Karen whose interest in me was far more romantic than mine in her. Stored in Karen's dad's hut for years, the ancient, rusting hulk would have been the pride of any mod raid on Brighton or, for that matter, Troon, back in the 1960s. In fact, so out of the way was our little Ayrshire backwater that even in 1970, when Dougie, then I, acquired the Vespa, throwback would-be Mods were arriving at the local school, Marr College, on Lambrettas festooned with mirrors and fake skunk tails. Later, some converted to Droogs, influenced by Stanley Kubrick's *A Clockwork Orange*, and used to parade about wearing white boiler suits and bowler hats. They smashed every window on the ground floor of the school on one occasion and I remember, as a nervous, be-blazered first-year, seeing one Droog belted on the jaw by our diminutive and extremely fiery Welsh headmaster.

A policeman standing near by was summoned by the large and outraged Droog. In a very un-Alex sort of way he shouted at the constable, 'See that? That bastard hit me! Arrest him.'

The policeman just shook his head. Those were the days. Any teacher trying such a thing now would be jailed for life and thrown out of the profession. And quite rightly so. Back then I was such a little middle-class establishment jerk I thought the rector was a hero, fighting the forces of evil.

The Vespa had no proper brakes, and the side-mounted engine made it essentially unstable. Nevertheless, I loved to tinker with its little two-stroke motor, decoking the head, adjusting the carburettor, listening to the ticking rip of its exhaust note and inhaling the sweet two-stroke tang.

At length it was sold to some mad third-years who wanted to ride it around Barassie Beach, and I acquired a Raleigh moped with no back brake. It cost £9, and was a bad, bad mistake. The frame had been twisted in an accident, and while it too provided a great smell of burnt two-stroke in the autumn air, it was soon out of favour. I sold it to the local Episcopalian vicar's son for a fiver and two bottles of Barr's Irn Bru. I didn't need it by then, because Dad had bought me a car.

The snag was, I couldn't drive it because, despite being seventeen, I hadn't even sat my driving test, let alone passed it. So I just used to start the cream-and-blue MG 1100, run it forward a few feet in first gear, then backwards, sit inside and smell the faint whiff of cigarette smoke, damp and old overheating. And dream of how much girls would be impressed by me, offering them lifts, leaning across, just . . . like . . . that to touch hair, cheek, face . . . no breasts. That was unthinkable. What breasts? Girls didn't have breasts!

Did they?

So I forgot that heady first love, motorbikes, and took driving lesson after driving lesson until I could perform three-point turns and reverse around corners without even blinking. I had memorised most of the Highway Code, knew my red triangles from my blue circles. I was ready. Ready to drive. Ready to enter the world of motorists. And as school ended, I went to Ayr, to the driving test centre near the race course, ready to begin my new life, so nervous, so afraid of failure, that I could barely speak. My mother sat beside me, her new blue leather coat and perfume filling the car with a strange smell which made me feel less than comforted. I couldn't smell the MG at all.

I was trembling with fear, anyway, and when asked to confirm my name and show my provisional licence, I didn't so much burble as bubble. A woman, or a sort of a woman, small, rotund, in a tightly belted raincoat and beret. This was the tester. She looked evil. She had a beard. But it was definitely a woman. We walked to a corner of the car park and she nodded to a distant Cortina. 'Please read that number plate,' she said, or something similar.

Oh no, I thought, I've gone blind. The number plate, normally well within the range of my unglassed eyes, swam and shimmered. My mouth was so full of saliva that I desperately needed to spit, while my throat, for some reason, was drier than an Iranian pub.

Get a grip, Tom, for goodness sake, I muttered inwardly, spilling some spittle. Swallowing disgustingly, my vision cleared and I read the number, feeling a sudden euphoria as the words emanating from my mouth appeared to be in English.

Soon we were climbing into the MG, me with my face hotter than the surface of the sun, she with her raincoat still belted, a clipboard held in front of her like a shield. Gloves. Black leather murderer's gloves. Not murderess's; murderer's. She had them on too.

The only thing I remember about the driving test was going straight through a give way sign without even pausing, and the sudden squawk of terror from the person on my left, followed by the handbrake being pulled on and the car sliding to halt, rather too late for safety. I mean, if anything had been coming, we would have been totalled anyway.

'Please drive back to the test centre, following my directions.'

'Does . . . does this mean I've failed?'

She made some shaky notes on her clipboard, and kept her eyes fixed there, well away from the tears I was so desperately trying to stop welling up in my eyes. 'Just follow my directions, please.'

Once I'd parked, in shell-shocked catatonia, she took her revenge by asking me, at length, a series of tedious questions from the *Highway Code*. I got them all wrong. And she wrote out the wrong colour of paper, the failing white, not the blessed green, handed it to me, grinning through her whiskers, and told me I had failed.

I walked on jellybaby legs to the café where my mother was waiting, and managed to walk her back to the car, handing her the keys on the way, before the storm of emotion broke, and hateful, horribly embarrassing, throat-swamping, nose-snuffling weeping ensued. I was seventeen, and a child at heart. I had failed the first test of manhood, and as Mum drove us home I felt bereft, as if the whole world had died except for me. Which in a way it had.

A whole summer lay ahead, the summer before university, and mobility had been denied me. Fantasies of sweeping girls off their feet and into my MG vanished, but there was a job waiting at Prestwick Airport, and somehow, morning by morning, shift by shift, I had to get there.

So I bought a motorbike. My third.

Well, sort of. To appease my anxious parents, it was a small motorbike. But not, I was at pains to point out, a moped.

One spring night, I travelled to one of Troon's suburban outposts and examined a Honda 50, one I remembered from school, which had been ridden slowly to classes each morning of her sixth year by a girl two years ahead of me, before she vanished into the mysteries of further education. It worked. I bought it. Twenty pounds, with the girl's father, official owner of the bike, knocking off a pound for good luck.

For a summer, I had a great time on that tiny, clutchless machine. A drama group I had been involved with at school clung together during the phoney holiday before uni, and two of them had diminutive bikes as well, all of us middle-class boys and girls, with protective parents determined not to allow us Triumphs or Nortons, just buzzy little passports to a small independence. We met for chips in Ayr, sneaked in, marginally under age, to hotel lounge bars.

Guilt stalked me like God, was God, as my religion still flourished in tandem with this tiny tilt at bohemianism. Each morning I would rattle and hum to Prestwick Airport where I provided passengers and crew with coffee, and sometimes more. There was one pilot, I remember, who would be supplied with surreptitious vodka in his morning brew by a kindly tea lady. Occasionally, coming for a change from the Ayr direction, and waiting to turn into the airport's entrance, and I would find myself looking over my shoulder, wondering if any cars, Ford Anglias perhaps, were hurtling towards me with murderous intent. But the mad Curly was nowhere to be seen. He had totalled the Anglia against a fence out near the Hillhouse Quarry, and been banned from driving as a result. Something in me felt considerably relieved.

Shift work at £12 a week took its toll. I took a job at a filling station, then a quarry, labouring. And I finally passed my driving test.

In the end it was easy. The same test centre in Ayr, a different examiner, male this time. Beardless. I breezed through the whole thing, and met my mother in that same café, unable to keep my face from a jaunty jaw-breaker of a smile. I tore off the L-plates, and later went to collect my sister from school, nonchalant and alone, for the first time, in the MG. I felt like a god, God help me.

And that was it for bikes, really, for thirteen years. Until my second wife began regaling me with tales of her bike-ridden past, the accidents on a bored-out MZ 125, the epic journeys back to Glasgow from Skye and Ireland, the boyfriend with a Triumph Trident 'Slippery Sam' racing replica. I began to feel a nagging need to show her that I too was capable of balancing a large lump of machinery between my legs. But, not having passed my motorcycle test, I had to make do with a Honda 125. Hey. Size isn't everything.

It was a CB 125T, to be precise, bought in Shetland during my stint as news editor of the local paper. Not having been on a bike for more than a decade, the first trip, home from the seller's croft, was a revelation. Despite the spring evening, it was bitterly cold. I felt a numbness creep deep into my being. And the borrowed full-face crash helmet (I'd only ever had open ones before) felt claustrophobic and scary. The bike, despite being a learner-legal piece of sweetness and light compared to some monsters, felt massive and in danger of falling over at any moment, crushing my spindly legs between it and the tarmac.

Not for the first time, nor the last, I decided to get fit, and abandoned motorcycling after a few months for the lung-pumping perils of pushbiking. But the infection had taken hold. I yearned for that rush of air into the face, the sense of powered flight which motorbikes bring. Effortless speed, being in the landscape, not separate from it. I was thinking Barry Sheene, Steve McQueen in *The Great Escape* (where, incidentally, the bike in that final jump suddenly turns from a wartime German BMW to a very post-war Triumph). So I bought an MZ combination.

Sidecars were then the only way of riding a bike of more than 125cc without having passed your test, and with the idea which would later become the book *Spirit of Adventure* (about driving round Scotland in search of the best whisky) glimmering in my cerebrum, I also surmised that (a) a bike with three wheels would stay upright more easily than a two-wheeled equivalent, should I find myself in any way damaged by noxious spirits and (b) the sidecar might come in handy for carting about any free samples. I was proved right on both counts, but not before I had undergone the alarming process of learning to ride a motorcycle combination. You have to steer them. Which may seem obvious, but on a proper bike, you don't steer, you just lean them round corners. A combination has to be battled around bends, in the MZ's case with the front wheel hopping and skipping like crazy, and sometimes with the sidecar three feet in the air. It was frightening for me and for anyone in the immediate vicinity, and if someone happened to be in the sidecar when it was three feet in the air, it often needed to be thoroughly disinfected afterwards.

Anyway, I survived. I underwent a three-day crash course and passed my test, strangely enough in Glasgow, in the area of the south side in which I'd been brought up. It was fun and easy, though I was surrounded by teenagers so pumped on adrenalin that they scared the innards out of me, and mid-life-crisis mothers looking for sex substitutes. Unlike me, a mid-life-crisis-ridden male looking for a sex substitute.

Then it was big-bike time. The Boanerges moment. But Brough Superiors were hard to find and a bit beyond my resources. Somehow, I couldn't stop the cheapskate dilettantism which afflicted my car buying, and I flitted from old beat-up monster to decayed beast: a Kawasaki Z650, which became the central character in the book *Hell's Golfer*. Then a Yamaha RD400E, a nutter's bike, a restored two-stroke flying machine which seized solid outside Nairn and sent me stupidly tumbling and unhurt in the ditch. A BMW R65 LS, a tarted-up boxer which would never start. I rode it from Glasgow to Inverness in a snowstorm and ended up taking two whole days to stop shivering. A very old and rusty Honda Goldwing which broke cables on every single trip, but which was like riding an armchair: 1100cc of half bike, half limousine.

The two bikes I own now are very different. One is the Triumph TR6, discreetly decaying in the garage, unridden for months and leaking oil like an incontinent pensioner. It is the bike I dreamed of when I was young and could never afford, or was never allowed to own by my parents. CVS: Classic Vehicle Syndrome. This coming winter I will finally get the old sod roadworthy, ready for one of the vintage rallies which happen frequently here in Shetland. And I will ride it like the boy I once was, proud, remembering, and happy.

But the other motorcycle in the household is used all the time as a means of achieving mental peace. For a sunny trip to the nearest newspaper shop, ten miles away, is a pleasure on a bike, removing cares, the required focus on just staying alive enough to drive away depression, however temporarily. The four-stroke MZ Skorpion is reliable and fun, if a little awkward for fat old idiots like myself. And uncomfortable: my wife has padded the seat out with extra foam, but I still get buttock cramps.

Sometimes I miss the old ring-ting-ting of the two-stroke engine which took me throughout Scotland in search of alcohol. I no longer drink and ride, though: the Skorpion is too fast to take chances on.

No more motorbikes. This is enough for me to play with. There are sufficient big boys' toys in this house. And it's dangerous. Some of my friends have faster, bigger machines, but as you age your reaction times slow, and something like a Suzuki Hayabusa (200 mph, 0–60 in two seconds) is just beyond my ability.

Besides, sometimes I find myself stopped at a junction, looking over my shoulder, particularly at night, wondering if that car bearing down on me too fast has really seen me, or if Curly is at the wheel, this time bent on genuine destruction.

So far he hasn't been.

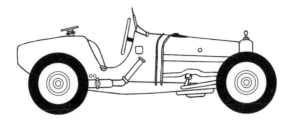

FORTY-THREE CARS AND TWELVE
MOTORCYCLES

Move. All I want to do is move; move on, have the landscape shuffling past, feel the world blowing past me like a breeze, a slipstream.

Or stay put. Home. I love my home, feel happy and secure there, but the urge to journey remains. To leave and return, leave and return. It's a male thing, maybe, built into the genes. At its most banal, it's there in the commuting life; it's why some men become so obsessive about what they do their commuting in or on: I'm off to the office to do some hunter-gathering, darling. And, God, am I a mean evil dangerous sex machine on my Ducati 916. Or my hand-built Orbit racing bike. My Vauxhall Cavalier SRI . . .

Leave and return, leave and return. Movement is such a drug, and the faster the speed of travelling, the more addictive, the more simultaneously thrilling and calming. Oh, the sheer pleasure of it! The joy! End of the working day, a still Glasgow summer's evening, fertile with possibility. A Kawasaki Z650, like the one Mel Gibson rode in the first *Mad Max* movie. The hot smell of leather and oil and petrol, the roar of replacement megaphone exhaust pipes. Blipping the throttle. That strange hiatus between city business and stillness, heat and chilling down, but not out. Things shifting. Movement. Movement to another place, another woman, another world. Even if it's just a five mile commute to the south side.

Happiness is movement; or travelling, having travelled, to have just arrived. That feeling of having achieved movement. In the strictly non-All-Bran sense. When journeying, there is no sense of frustration, of defeat. Not unless you are in some way stopped, stranded, stuck. You may be running away from something, or towards a destination full of hope and possibility. Alone in a car or on a motorbike you have control, you are your own master, and master of the machine. And on a bike, too, there is the constant, edgy, delightful threat of imminent death. In a train or an aeroplane, your fate is in someone else's hands. Somebody other than yourself has to deal with those leaves on the line, that burning engine. No control. No direction home. Not really.

On your own, with that internal combustion engine in front, behind, between your legs, you're testing yourself. On a bike it's distilled, concentrated: you're moving, living, feeling the possibility of your own demise in every turn, every extra mile per hour. On a bike it's there.

One foot down on the road and you're off. Minced. But in a car, things can go wrong too. One flick of the steering wheel to the left and you're through the barrier and plummeting from the Kingston Bridge towards the festering Clyde, thinking to yourself: oops. Your whole life flashing before you. Splash.

History: it's movement, change. And movement is life.

All my life, cars and bikes have been the sources of happiness, the contexts in which joys and sometimes tragedies have been worked out, played out. If I was American, I'd say something Springsteenian, like, the road, man: that's my destiny. Well, in the British Isles there just isn't the landscape for that kind of widescreen dreaming. Our roads are small, short, narrow; our horizons are limited. We are bound by the sea on every side. When Paddy McAloon of Prefab Sprout sang, in riposte to the Great Bruce, life is more, much more than cars and girls, what he really meant was, here in squashed wee Britain cars cannot take us far enough, out into the wide open spaces of the midwest. Here we can't really 'Drive All

Night', there's no 'Racing In The Streets'. Strapping your best girl's hands across your engines would be painful, probably. And cold.

These days home is on an island where I am never any more than two miles from the sea. And maybe I like that, now. Maybe I want that sense of being bound. As long as I can get on a plane or a boat occasionally, and find a new continent waiting somewhere. Just to test myself, just to leave and return. Move.

I'm sitting in a court room, in the press benches, waiting endlessly for the sheriff to return from his luxuriously appointed private quarters to make a decision. That's a Scottish sheriff, by the way, not an American tin-star cowboy Randolph Scott sort of sheriff. This sheriff comes in wig, gown and starched white collar straight from the eighteenth century. A judge, in other words.

You don't want to know about the case, it's turgid and tedious and nasty. There is an argument involving something called *adminiculation*, which means to decide on the balance of probabilities given the limited, if best available, evidence.

To occupy myself, to fight off the spine-melting boredom, I'm listing cars on a sheet of notepaper, doodling names, memories, colours, smells: MG 1100. First car: smelt of victory, of mobility, of the sheer and absolute joy of passing my driving test. There had been bikes before, but this . . . this was social. This was sex; broke the car's back by piling seven students into it. Not for sex. For mobility. Social mobility.

Fiat 500: smashed into the back of a Ford Zephyr; three-inch scar on my forehead still, red and sometimes inflamed. On my way to see the re-run of *Gone With the Wind* at the old ABC in Sauchiehall Street. Dad rebuilt the ruined little Cinquecento, but it never felt same. Especially given the fact that he accidentally resprayed it pink. First heavy petting experience happened within its cramped environs. Mini Clubman Estate.

Burst the petrol tank on the M8. Once slept in it at Lorient in France. No suspension to speak of.

And on and on: Wolseley 2200 (why? Size isn't everything; one side of the hydropneumatic suspension deflated itself near Wick), Ford Escort Estate (a gift in aid of my Christian service as a singing evangelist; see *Red Guitars in Heaven* for further false information) VW Beetle (so rotten it only lasted a month before the front end collapsed in on itself), Fiat 127 (eaten internally by a bearded collie called Dylan), Citroën 2CV (divorce sparked by faulty igniton), Honda Civic (cheap from a hi-fi shop I briefly worked for; noisiest tappets in history), Fiat 131 Mirafiori (sold with no brakes, no clutch and nearly no oil), Renault 11 (rebuilt by a dodgy garage in Maryhill using bits of plastic cardboard), Ford Cortina Estate (swapped for typewriter with girlfriend), MG Maestro (repossessed), Colt Sigma Estate (rusted to a brown nothing, but still started at the first turn), Renault 4 (*Shetland Times* company car), BMW 520 (sold to Unst teenage racer for peanuts), Volkswagen Golf (second wife's car; demolished in high-speed Shetlandic accident involving sheep), Volvo 340LS (oh God, add the LS; don't imagine it was a bog standard 340, please! It was metallic black and handled like a dog on acid), Ford Escort again (company car from *The Scotsman*, written off by a stray deer near Lochinver).

Replaced by a Peugeot 309 Diesel called a Style, which must have been ironic; then there were the campers, heaven and hell, but mostly hell: three VWs and an imported Fiat. Given half a chance, I'd buy another camper tomorrow, but it would mean another divorce.

Mercedes 230E, bought stupidly; I was seduced by that radiator star, ripped off by an octogenarian con merchant from Nairn. Vauxhall Astra Estate: ripped off by a mechanic who offered to swap the Astra for the Merc, as it would 'cost too much to fix it'. Ford Escort RS Turbo: my first and most successful book bought this for my wife. It was psychotically ugly and naff, but insanely fast, and had to have VR-rated tyres capable of handling 150 mph – a speed easily reached, though the speedometer may have spoken with forked tongue. Citroën Saxo, brand new. And here we come to the reason I hate Citroëns so much: third breakdown, the mechanic just shrugs and says, 'Sometimes you just get a bad one.' I make Citroën take it back. By dumping it in the garage forecourt with a note and the keys. They don't argue.

Audi 80: fine until the sun roof opened and fell into a heap of rust. The car became a permanent convertible. Lancia Delta: looked great, was basically blue-painted rust and plastic padding. Fiat Panda 4X4: turned out it had been salvaged from the sea. You could smell the salt in its innards. Nissan Patrol (a lumbering, belching, characterless lorry with the road manners of a water buffalo), Skoda Rapide (poor man's Porsche, they said. Ha!), Fiat Cinquecento (mad plans to save money), Volvo 340 (bought for £500 as a runaround while working in Glasgow one summer; described by the main dealer as 'terminally diseased'; stolen, thank goodness), Toyota Carina CDX (comfort with tedium), Peugeot 406 Turbo Diesel (a great, absolutely boring car, impossible to see out of in wet weather), Toyota HiLux crew-cab pick-up (utter, monstrous redneck reliability) . . . and now the Land Rover.

Forty-three cars. Forty-three cars owned. All human, or nearly human, life is there. All the tears, tantrums, children, women, pals. Breakdowns, driving drunk and sober, bad destinations, depressed journeys into blind nowhere . . . and delight. Delight in movement. In leaving and returning.

Most of those cars were real rustbuckets, too. Only in the past few years have I been able to afford even modestly respectable transport. Yet I've thrown away a fortune on fantasies like that Mercedes, and the BMW. Don't even ask about running and repair costs. Ironically, in the past three years I've become a sort of motoring pundit, presenting a telly show about cars and bikes, and I get to drive and ride the best and the most beautiful, all for nothing. You really have to laugh. I do.

At the Sheriff Court, the jury's still out.

How about bikes? The first motorcycle, if you can call it that, I was ever on belonged to my friend and neighbour Dougie Walker. It was the ancient Vespa 150 scooter, rusty and apparently deceased, engine-wise, when Dougie got it. A degree of spark-plug cleaning and general bashing

INTERNAL COMBUSTION

71

with hammers eventually had the thing puttering noisily through its holed silencer, and as Dougie and I were still just fourteen, we decided to take it motocrossing in the woods behind his house. Never mind that scooters, with their tiny wheels, low running boards and inherent instability, are hardly the thing for jumping and leaping from rutted path to rocky hillock. Not a jot or a tittle did we care, as helmetless we thundered – well, plootered – along narrow winding paths, scaring pensioners into incipient heart failure and eventually annoying Dougie's parents so much that he was forced to get rid of the Vespa.

So I bought it. For the princely sum of £3.50. Our house, on the opposite side of Ottoline Drive from Dougie's, backed onto the three municipal golf courses, Lochgreen, Darley and Fullerton, and so it seemed natural to race the Vespa up and down the fairways. I was, along with nearly every other inhabitant of Troon, a golfer myself, or at least a teenage hacker whose enthusiasm outpaced his skill. So I was sensitive to the greens, trying to avoid leaving skid marks or ruts wherever possible. But, as I've said, we did enjoy doing jumps off the tops of bunkers.

Of course, golfers were a bit of a hazard, but we (Dougie was happy to swap the trees for rough and greensward) tended to take the scooter out in twilight, and few wielders of niblick or mashie were left to bother us as we conducted our dangerous wheelie leaps, the tiny side-mounted Italian engine squealing like a tortured rabbit. Sometimes, in the half-light, we did come tremendous croppers, colliding painfully with gorse bushes or failing to notice a looming bunker entirely. Somehow, we and the scooter survived, almost undamaged.

Such antics could not pass unnoticed, of course, and a few local residents began to complain about the watery headlight and two-stroke howling out on the wastes of the linksland. Everyone knew it was us, and we were nice middle-class boys, but still I think we were fortunate that the police were never called. However, there were one or two narrow escapes from the rangers employed to roam the course checking that green fees had been paid, one or two of whom occasionally lurked on into the gloaming. And, in the end, I was told in no uncertain terms by my father that too many tyre marks were being left on the Lochgreen greens. I blamed it on the greenkeepers' tractors, but the difference between their tyre size and mine was noticeable, decidedly. Still, the memories linger on, and to this day I cannot look at a golf course without wistfully wondering what it would be like to jump a diseased Italian scooter off that particular tee, or go roaring up a narrow fairway and perform a skid turn on a pristine green. I was almost overcome by these thoughts recently when making a radio programme at Royal Lytham, which to my mind would be improved by a bit of attention with motorcycles. Say, a weekend motocross meet.

Anyway, sixteen, and legal motorcycling was approaching. Dougie, a bit older than me, had bought a BSA Bantam, which looked just like a real motorbike and, at 175cc, almost was one. It belched blue fumes as, sporting L-plates (you could ride anything up to 250cc in those days on a provisional) he sedately whirred to and from school, helmetless. Sometimes he would deign to pick me up, but pillion travel tended to slow the thing to walking pace, and it was nothing like as exciting as tree-avoidance or bunker-hopping aboard the Vespa.

I sold the Vespa and acquired what I hoped would soon be the road-legal Raleigh moped. As well as its twisted frame, it turned out to have no back brake; while this held no terrors for me, the MOT examiner, or mechanic, if you will, at the Cooper Brothers' garage was not so sanguine. Asked if it was strictly necessary for a moped to have a back brake, he looked at me with a kind of pitying leer. And pointed out the twist in the frame.

About this time, I fell out with Cooper Brothers after Les discovered Dougie and me in the workshop, trying to buy a James 200 from the said MOT examiner-cum-mechanic, who ran a thriving used bike business from under his employer's nose. Les chased us, limping and furious. God knows what happened to the mechanic. If he did get the sack, it was all he deserved for refusing to give my brakeless Raleigh an MOT.

I then bought the aforementioned Honda 50, hacksawed the last four inches from the silencer of Mr Honda's multi-million-selling masterpiece, and there began that summer of 35 to 40 mph thrashing along the back roads of Ayrshire. It was bliss. I felt like Peter Fonda or Dennis Hopper in *Easy Rider*, a film I had never seen – my parents were religiously strict on X-rated films for under-eighteens, or indeed for anyone, and I had a strong feeling I would be struck down dead by God should I enter a cinema on such a nefarious mission anyway. Hanging out with my local drama group, I felt the stirrings of lust for a fifteen-year-old classmate of my sister's, an actress of style and sexiness who looked all of twenty-seven. But on the Honda, screeching from Ayr Civic Theatre to the Sun Court Hotel, where they would let us drink under-age, I could not compete with my vicar's son, the one who had bought my Raleigh for £3.50 and two bottles of Irn Bru, who was now fully equipped with an Austin 1300. It looked the same as my MG, except my radiator grille was much sexier. But the 1100 lay shrouded in the garage, immobile, awaiting road-going legality on my part.

A friend who, like me, had a student job at the airport, rode a Honda 50 as well. He had stripped it of leg guards and side panels so that it resembled a kind of one dimensional pram. Claiming he could get 50 mph out of it, he would race me around South Woods and, our engines whining like baby banshees, we would throw the bikes over on their sides until sparks flew from the foot rests, and I could tell that nothing would ever get either bike above 40. Not a hurricane at our tails. Nothing.

As the summer drew to a close, Stephen, one of the actors in the drama group, bought a Honda 90 sport, a mean little black thing which could outstrip either Honda 50 by many miles per hour. The week I finally passed my car test, he crashed it into a van on the way to an appointment at my dad's dental surgery, seriously injuring himself, and my mum ragingly informed me I would never ride a motorbike again, not in her house. Not that I had ever actually ridden a bike indoors anyway. Stephen eventually recovered. I sold the Honda for £25 and didn't sit astride another motorbike for a decade and a half.

I returned to biking in my mid-thirties, a sad statistic, typical of many middle-aged 'returnees', as the trade calls them, desperately seeking what

Philip Larkin calls 'the sickening breathlessness of being young'. Partly, it was unfinished business. I had never passed my bike test, never ridden anything large and fast. Thunder Road beckoned. But my envy of Stewart still haunted my mind.

Because if Dougie Walker went on to become a lawyer and abandoned bikes, Stewart left school at fifteen, took up an apprenticeship as a toolmaker, and quickly acquired the biggest and fastest bikes of anybody I knew. His first, pre-test machine was a Honda CD250; after that, he moved quickly on to a BSA Gold Star, so unashamedly, nakedly, brutally fast it made you wince to see it, with its clip-ons and sports saddle. There were Triumphs too, and a Kawasaki, I think.

In addition, but not instead of all this, he bought an old and rotting Jaguar saloon. I still remember the ignominy with which I was forced to turn down the offer of a pillion ride on Stewart's Honda, immediately after he'd passed his test and could legally carry passengers. It was to see, you've guessed it, *Easy Rider* at the Odeon in Ayr, and at first I told my mum I was going with Stewart on the train to see 'a film'. Being truthful by nature (and also very concerned about divine zapping) I eventually revealed that we planned to go to an X-rated movie and on board Stewart's bike. The shriek of rage could be heard on the other side of the golf course.

Stewart went to Australia and we lost touch until quite recently, when he looked me up during a trip back to the UK. He hadn't changed at all. He had a couple of bikes – I think one of them was, inevitably, a Kawasaki ZZR1100, at that time, before the advent of the Suzuku Hayabusa, the fastest production motorbike you could buy – and he had run the gamut of bikedom in the intervening years from Goldwings to Fireblades. He was as cool and self-possessed as I remembered, telling tales of Turkish baths in the natural steam of opal mines, chopping down trees in Queensland with an AK47 semi-automatic rifle. And he wanted to know what kind of bike I had. I had an MZ 250, four hundred quid's worth. Big deal.

And of course, I still have an MZ, or to be precise an MuZ, and the

Skorpion Sport which is the mechanical love of my life is lurking at home in a dank garage surrounded by sheep and silage.

I barely ride my two motorbikes, of course. It's too cold, I'm too old. And, besides, that leaving and returning thing? I find I like the returning bit more and more. Having returned alive.

The jury's coming back in. The clerk is bustling around, ready to call the sheriff. A verdict. But I'm looking at these scrawled lists of cars and bikes, and realising just how much these are the icons of my life, the signifiers of existence, the containers of lust and love, hopes and dreams, images of success and failure, happiness and hatred. It's a life not on the road, but in-car, on bike. Mobility. Freedom. Freedom to leave, and then come home again. Because you can.

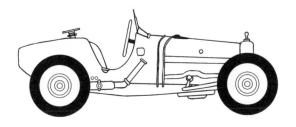

THE CARAVAN IS ON ITS WAY

always think,' said my much younger, much cooler, much singler friend, 'that there's something ineffably sad about people who go caravanning.'

I nodded sagely and cracked open another tin of Belhaven Best. I had just bought a caravan. A Trophy Olympic Gold caravan, twelve years old, sixteen feet nine inches of fake oak, swirling carpets and seat covers calculated to give a blind man a migraine.

'I've just bought a caravan,' I said, as beer bubbled over aluminium.

My pal grinned in the glassy fashion which indicates feverish behind-the-eyes activity of the what-the-hell-can-I-possibly-say variety. 'Ah,' he said. 'Any chance of another beer?'

'Nope,' I replied, 'I need it to alleviate my central, ineffable sadness, and render me as temporarily happy as is possible, given my newly caravanised circumstances.'

Caravans and their slightly cooler cousins, camper vans, have haunted my life, continual temptations in my mobility, offering all the very real attractions of the gypsy lifestyle. For the independent itinerant in us all, there is something wonderful about carrying your own home around with you. And tents, given the vicissitudes of British weather, just don't cut it when it comes to keeping the rain, snow, hail, plagues of frogs or falling trees off. Leaving aside entirely the question of erection, as the small-time porn actress said to the corpulent government minister.

I too have gone through my caravans-are-for-saddos phase, but I have now emerged, all the sadder for being glad to own the Trophy, with its electric hook-up, water heater, shower, chemical toilet, rollable water barrel, four-burner cooker, oven and auto-reverse brakes. Its double glazing, built-in stereo, cut moquette upholstery and awning. For it means I do not have to take the family around a series of youth hostels crammed with youth, much of it foreign and sweaty, and the elderly, who come to youth hostels, it seems, to die, as was originally mooted by my other half.

And my heart is light within me at the thought of being crammed into the luxurious but undoubtedly limited space of the Trophy for ten days, which will take in the promised theme parks and films, London and Hadrian's Wall. For the memories of childhood caravan holidays have undergone the filtration process of middle-aged adulthood, by which unpleasantness, pain, frustration and sorrow are removed, leaving only the glow of nostalgia.

I suppose I could have bought – yet another – camper van or, if you will, motorhome. But having the Land Rover, with its almost unlimited towing capacity, suddenly made me realise that we could go just as fast with a lump of fibreglass, aluminium and fake oak hooked up behind as without. And when you buy a camper, unless it's something newish costing upwards of fifteen grand, you are potentially entering a world of pain. Those agonies are too fresh to have been transformed into misty-eyed memory. I mean, you only have to break down, in your mobile wheeled palace, inside the lion enclosure at a safari park to have the experience etched forever in scar tissue on your brain . . . the trembling in your hands stops, in the end. Unless you let yourself remember too much . . .

Vomit is my earliest, agonisingly retrieved memory of travelling in a caravanette, as we called it then. My vomit and my sister's. We were in the back, unbelted of course, of some kind of horrible, wobbly, top-heavy Bedford, which Dad had hired to take us from Glasgow to a church camp down at Carradale on the Kintyre peninsula. I must have been about five, my sister three. There was a distinctive smell which I think set us off. A weird, plasticky, shiny aroma, and petrol. In those days, cars were expected to leak a bit. To leak everything – petrol, oil, water, exhaust. I'm still haunted today by the tragic death of the late Sir Nicholas Fairbairn's baby son in the back of a van, due to carbon monoxide poisoning from a holed exhaust. I used to love the smell of exhaust fumes.

Anyway, my parents put up with the Bedford's various niffs, piled us loosely into the back amid blankets and newly purchased sleeping bags, and off we went, up Loch Lomondside on a road so twisty then (and now) that it can induce motion sickness in a stuffed aardvark. We were stuffed only with rolls and square sliced (Lorne) sausage, which quickly reappeared, somewhat masticated and part-digested. Which only made the Bedford smell worse.

Somehow, I can't recall anything about the sleeping arrangements, though things must have been tight. Nor have many memories survived of our next camper van trip, this time to Southend in a Volkswagen Caravette, also hired, which had an even worse smell than the Bedford (due, no doubt, to the heat exchangers which VW used to turn their exhaust pipes into heaters, and which later seemed to me a gassing accident waiting to happen) and a more oceanic motion too. It would have been one of the very first, split-screen Type Two (the Beetle was Type One) campers, and worth a fortune these days if it could be magically revivified. We were sick again. Square sliced sausages? Can't remember. I do, however, know that we stopped at one point for mutton pies supplied by a bakery and that they were so greasy each pie (round, known in Scotland as an ashet, or container-like, pie) had half an inch of liquid fat penned within its pastry borders. I drank and ate. No wonder my cholesterol is high.

With everyone getting bigger and another sister duly delivered, Dad decided that the compact and bijou nature of camper vans was no longer on for the Morton family. And, presumably, he was sick of the sickness. However, he was hooked on the notion of self-contained holidays, and so the following summer we hired a caravan, and headed off for the Highlands in the Hillman Super Minx Estate, a strange, pitched-roof thing trailing behind us. Hills were hard. The Minx strained to cart the heavy burden behind us up romantically named roads, like the Rest And Be Thankful and the Devil's Elbow. Little survives in my cerebral cortex of what life within the caravan was actually like, but I do remember being outraged that we weren't allowed to travel in it. Instead, we children perched on the Minx's slippery red back seat, gazing out at the thing behind us, waiting for it to disengage and go hurtling into the line of lorries and cars toiling behind it.

One thing I do remember. This van was some kind of 1950s remnant, and it came complete with the social mores and rigid puritanism of its time built into the fabric of its interior. When we went to bed, the children were packed like sardines onto a platform made from bits of table and bench seats in classic caravan style. But then, a complex arrangement of boards and sliding screens was bolted into place to seal us off from the adult half of the van, which included the door to the outside world and freedom. And for that matter, toilets. For this was before carrying your own Porta-Potti had become acceptable. Peeing and pooing had to be done well out of earshot and indeed nose shot of any easily offended person. And everyone was easily offended in the early '60s.

It was with horror that and I my sister (the baby was granted a reprieve and kept within breast-feeding distance on the Other Side) were sealed off by a blank board wall from our parents. It was like being walled up for the night. And there was no light. Both of us were used to having a lamp left on at home, at least in the corridor, with our bedroom door left slightly ajar. But this! This was awful, a pit of darkness pierced by the frustrating spill of gas-mantle illumination from Beyond the Board. The wind caught our van and rocked it, creakingly. Strange, damp, smoky smells wafted from beneath our rapidly mildewing pillows. Rain spattered against

INTERNAL COMBUSTION

80

windows and roof, and in the morning we would wake with our faces soaked in dripping condensation.

Once I woke, screaming, in the still, utterly complete darkness of pre-dawn. There was a scuffling and a crashing from the other side of the now-invisible barrier which separated us from our parents. My sister was awake now, too, crying with supportive intensity. Suddenly, with a clatter, the barrier dividing the van crashed down, and as my mother drowsily pointed a torch, Dad scraped matches and lit, with a soft whoomp, the gas light, filling the caravan with a soft yellow comforting glow, the smell of extinguished Swan matches, and the adenoidal hiss of burning gas.

Today, it's still one of the most comforting aromas I can imagine. Recreating it is hard, though lighting the Rayburn in our house comes close. And we have a couple of Camping Gaz lights which make something approaching the same sound. You have to lean in close to catch a whiff of that remembered odour, though. It's the smell of salvation, the arrival of protection, the reassurance that those you love have not deserted you.

When we returned home to Glasgow, the Hillman needed a new clutch, and the caravan hirer took great delight in showing my father that he'd had the beast's handbrake on for the entire duration of the trip. Never again, said my mother. Two years later, Dad bought a caravan.

It was called a Sprite Musketeer, and it had an odd Coke-bottle kink in its roofline. It was a pale, lemony yellow, and had a kind of austere modernity the ancient '50s thing which had destroyed the Super Minx's clutch did not possess. There were no solid barriers dividing up the interior at night, only a curtain. By this time Dad had also acquired a much more potent lump of Luton tin, a Vauxhall Cresta, and we were set for the long haul: this rig was continent-bound.

At nine or so, I was old enough to take an interest in the whole macho culture of caravan-tending and manoeuvring. I took delight in winding up the jockey heel, lowering the stabilisers when we stopped for the night, even switching on the Calor gas. I helped Mum and Dad as they pushed and pulled the yellow van – so cheaply made that I can remember its aluminium body panels flexing in the wind like sails – in and out of our driveway, and it was my job to install at every stop the little metal step which made entering the Sprite easier. That was how we lost about four of them, as Dad drove off with the step left on its own in a lay-by or campsite.

We had to have a few dry runs, of course, before venturing abroad, somewhere neither Dad nor Mum had ever been. We went to Oban, to the all-tarmac site of Ganavan Sands. To the Lake District for a long weekend, where the rain was so heavy it dented the Muskateer's none-too-solid roof. And Portpatrick, where Dad left my mother and her three offspring for a week while he went back to work.

And I learned to love that caravan. It seems now that I was outside all the time, running, digging, making dams in forest streams, climbing trees, swinging on old frayed ropes over deep rivers. The smells are with me still: the damp steaminess of rain-soaked anoraks slowly drying. The keen sharp tang of gas, the stunning sensation of waking to frying bacon. The odd, dried-glue background smell which was and will forever be Sprite. And, latterly, the choking, antiseptic, bleachy, gagging horror of the chemical toilet, which was only ever used in emergencies and was sealed beneath a metal lid so heavy my dad needed two hands to lift it. At night, sometimes, we would be wakened by the splashing thump of gigantic adult shits – or, as they were universally known in those days, jobbies – being perpetrated in the toilet compartment a centimetre from our childish heads. That is not a smell I relish recalling.

At last the summer's day came when we headed off to the mystery and wonder of France, surging down the A roads and occasional bits and pieces of that newfangled thing, the motorway, to Southampton, where we were to catch the Townsend Thoresen ferry to Cherbourg.

Never has so much vomit been produced by so few people. The voyage was meant to take six hours, I think. It lasted eight. A force-eight gale battered the boat with a ferocity none of us had ever felt or imagined. Wind, in our city and suburban lives, was something caused by too much cauliflower. My sisters just sicked up everything and moaned. My mother went chalk white and groaned. Dad booked a cabin while I, nine, fearless and nausea-free, ran about the upper deck in the wind and spray until I accidentally found myself downwind of an elderly man throwing up his breakfast and, presumably, four or five other meals as well. I caught the lot full in the face. And found that sea-sickness can be infectious.

But when we got off the boat and recovered our equilibrium, the holiday was an absolute delight. For the first time in my life I saw my parents drinking wine. We children discovered the extraordinary tastes of French cheeses, fresh fruits we could only dream about back home, lemonade which filled the mouth with bubbles and something other than chemical scum. We stayed in Breton campsites breathtakingly well equipped with everything from swimming pools to circus trapezes, effortlessly made friends with French kids, and ignored almost completely that this was 1968, and the fact that France, not to mention Youth, was on the rampage.

Sometimes I look back on that time and wonder about the world going half-crazy on drugs, rock'n'roll and politics, while we caravanned slowly about Brittany and had the best holiday of our lives. What was I doing in 1968? Playing pinball on a machine in a Les Moutiers bar, racing down to the beach, snorkelling in mud, harvesting prawns and eating them for the first time, discovering that steak could be red in the middle, and wondering why the French had bread and we had Milanda. Nothing would ever be the same again.

Well, apart from the fact that we went caravanning every summer, Easter and October holiday for year after year after year. The Muskateer was traded in for a whopping great Sprite Major, a vast eighteen feet long, the Cresta for a new model and then a succession of Fords. The second Cresta broke down somewhere near Lyon, but we didn't care. We towed that Sprite all the way to the Costa Brava, staying on a massive, enormously busy site called Cala Go Go near Playa De Aro. It was hotter than I had believed possible. We slept fitfully in the Sprite, all the windows open, while booming pop songs reverberated from the beachfront disco. *We skipped the light fandango, turned cartwheels 'cross the floor* . . . what was that about? And wasn't that from ages ago, anyway?

We went for Easter breaks where our cheeks froze to the sides of the van during the night, and nobody minded. Once, in Keswick, there was six inches of snow on the ground. I had my first driving lesson aged fifteen on the perimeter track of the Bassenthwaite site, in what Dad was using then to tow the now-decaying Major: a Morris 1800 Special, that dismal, diseased landcrab. And, as described in full scatological detail in the book *Spirit of Adventure*, the event occurred which marked the end of my enjoyment of caravan holidays. At sixteen, there was the Great Toilet Disaster of North Ledaig, near Oban, when a mis-timed visit to the caravan site toilets resulted in my being posted missing for several hours, until rescued by a worried father bearing clean clothes and two loo rolls.

Caravans and adolescence do not mix. There is no room for hormones to rampage in the proper manner aboard even the largest touring caravan. So we moved on to rented holiday apartments and, as the family grew and began to leave home, the Major mouldered, then was traded in for a smaller, three-berth van, one I was rarely in and which remains white, anonymous and, in memory, entirely odour-free.

I would never, I swore, go on holiday in a caravan again. And I never did. Well, not until now. Not until the Trophy Olympic Gold.

Unless, of course, you count camper vans.

It began with a Volkswagen, and it was a style thing, really. I was living in the village of Cromarty, in the Black Isle, north of Inverness, working for *The Scotsman*, and had just made a bit of cash from writing the official (rather too official, in hindsight) biography of a band called Runrig. A friend was completely besotted with all things vintage and VW, and while I couldn't justify a restored Beetle, what with a company car not to worry about, a camper was on the cards. At that stage we had two kids and it offered, just as it had my father, the chance of mobile accommodation.

But it had to be a VW. Volkswagen campers had credibility, you see, reaching back into the '60s, when Arlo Guthrie's *Alice's Restaurant* song-cum-movie revolved around the central icon of counter-culture transport, the VW Microbus. They travelled the world, were still in the late '80s the favoured means of getting from Australia to the UK, if you were five or six surfers looking for work in Camden Town as barkeeps, and lasted, so it was said, forever. I began looking.

The first VW camper I saw had in fact come from Australia. It was a left-hand drive, and had done 170,000 miles.

'It might be 270,000, actually,' said the owner. 'Or even just 70,000. I bought it from the guy who drove it here from Sydney, and he said it was on its third engine. It's a 1600. Actually, I think it's kilometres, not miles. And the speedo's broken.'

The camper drove reasonably well, and had one of those pop-up roofs. It had a slightly decayed smell, though, presumably due to the exuded perspiration of large Aussies as they made their way through Afghanistan or some such place. I agreed to buy it for £1,400, and promised to return in two days with the money. My wife nearly decked me when I told her.

'You just throw cash away,' she said (something she still tells me all too frequently), 'and this is something we're all going to have to stay in, not just you. I want to see it.' And so we drove out to Drumnadrochit, on the shores of Loch Ness, where the seller lived. While Susan fulminated, her face set pretty much as I imagine Tam o' Shanter's missus nursing her wrath to keep it warm, I explained that we'd like another look at the camper.

'It smells,' announced my esteemed partner, as she examined the stained upholstery and (I could see now) torn plastic of the elevating roof, 'like something died in here'.

The owner looked at me questioningly: I thought we had a deal, his expression said. I felt myself visibly shrinking. Heartily, I laughed. Too heartily.

'Has my husband given you any money?'

The surprised camper-possessor shook his head.

'Good, because he isn't going to.' I was aghast. In all our years of knowing each other, Susan had never acted in such a fashion. It was clear we would have to divorce instantly.

The seller sighed. 'Ah well, you're probably right,' he said. 'It is a pile of shite, really. I wouldn't have liked you and a baby to have to sleep in there. It took a long time to get the hen crap cleaned off the seats.'

We drove back to Cromarty in silence. I was a chastened man. Slightly.

But somehow the magic of VW campers had taken mild possession of Susan, and it was only a week or two before she had located, in Cromarty, a yellow, much better equipped, newer, right-hand drive and thoroughly un-Australian vehicle. It was a whopping £2,500, but it had a fridge, and the kind of elevating roof which makes the van concerned look like a dead accordion.

We went away in the Yellow Peril exactly twice. Once to Applecross, a beautiful but isolated village on the west coast of Scotland, where we were bitten so badly by midges that I thought I was going to have to self-amputate my feet, and Susan's face swelled up in an allergic reaction so that she looked like she was suffering from some dreadful tropical skin condition. And once to Shetland, where we lasted a week before a friend took pity on us and gave us her house while she went away on holiday.

But that wasn't the end of the Yellow Peril. Oh no. I used it for one *Scotsman* assignment, travelling way up into Sutherland to interview Rebecca Ridgeway, the amazingly beautiful, if somewhat intimidating, daughter of long-distance rower John. I parked the van at the beginning of the rugged footpath which leads into the Ridgeways' remote retreat, an adventure holiday centre for corporate types needing to sort out their leadership skills by building rafts from old oil-drums, and nonchalantly took my newly acquired mountain bike from the rack. Never having cycled off-road in my life, I managed about half a mile before hitting a tree root, cart-wheeling over the handlebars and leaving the front forks utterly wrecked.

When I finally arrived on John Ridgeway's doorstep, he was unamused: 'What sort of time do you call this?' he boomed, then wandered up to the strange glass tower from where he surveys his kingdom – a very nice tree- and water-bound glen, a sort of Lost Kingdom of Sweat. 'Take your shoes off. Rebecca'll be here in a minute.'

She was. She served me homemade scones and tea. I interviewed her (she was just about to canoe around the Arctic, as one does if one is a Ridgeway), fell in love, and walked back to my bent bike. Which I had to carry back to the camper. Love faded.

I spent the night in Scourie, an unfeasibly lovely spot where Rod Stewart once shagged Britt Ekland. I drank Stella Artois and felt the wind heel the camper like a boat.

There was more. We decided to move back to Shetland from Cromarty, to a house which was in a state of disrepair, not to say dereliction. So I volunteered, having resigned from *The Scotsman*, to take the camper north, squat there for a month and help the builders make the house habitable. It was January.

Having landed safely, if somewhat discombobulated, in Shetland after the fourteen-hour sea trip from Aberdeen (that cross-channel force eight was nothing; on the Shetland run you get used to near-hurricanes), I drove the Yellow Peril north to our house-cum-building site, loaded down with everything you can imagine, and some you probably can't. Including two goldfish and a spare kitchen sink. Five miles from my destination, a stone smashed the windscreen. The gales of the previous night had not abated, so the wind immediately cascaded safety glass all over my lap, and indeed the goldfish. A gust caught the van and suddenly it felt like I was airborne. The entire VW lifted into the air and was slammed down on the other side of the road, wheels askew. I turned around. The elevating accordion roof had, well, elevated, and was even now ballooning above me, filled with the icy northern blast of a Shetland gale. At any moment I was going to be tumbled into the sea.

I stopped, managed to lower the roof and secured it as best I could. My eyes streaming, face hammered by wind and bits of stray glass, I drove to the house. When I unloaded, the goldfish were dead. Some fish are not meant to fly.

For the next month, life was strange. I squatted in the unheated, unplumbed house, spending the nights inside two sleeping-bags, while mice ran over my face, sometimes even waking me up. No replacement windscreen being immediately available, I taped a salvaged Morris Minor rear window onto the VW and sealed it with damp-proof-course polythene sheeting. I could see virtually nothing, but drove anyway. The brakes seized. Comprehensively insured as the VW was, I contemplated arson. But instead, spring came, Susan arrived, the van was repaired at vast expense and sold to an eighteen-year-old acne-ridden chap who told me bluntly that he wanted it so he and his girlfriend could 'take drugs and have sex'. I let him drive the Yellow Peril away for £700. And swore that never, never, never ever would I buy another.

But stuff happened.

What happened was a sudden career in broadcasting. It was the Law of Sod that, having moved to Shetland (back to Shetland; we had abandoned the place only four years previously), I should be offered a contract presenting a daily radio show by the BBC. The only problem was that the show had to come from Inverness, just a spit away from our former home in the Black Isle. But a plane, taxi, train and another taxi ride from Shetland. One way.

There was a good reason for doing it, though, despite the stranding of my wife and weans (up to three now) in the middle of the North Sea. We didn't have a toilet. And we didn't have any money. Actually, we did have a sort of toilet, a Swedish electric composing bio-loo which was supposed to turn shite and piss into dried, powdered compost, but it had never worked properly since my mother-in-law had used it once every half hour for five days, filling it with three gallons of pee, fusing the electrics and solidifying the supposedly powdered compost into a horrendous, rock-hard mass.

So I went to Inverness, for four days every week. At first I rented a flat in the Queen of the Highland Fleshpots, and then one in nearby Nairn. But in the end I grew to dislike the idea of having two homes, and decided to render one of them temporary. It was a kind of masochism, I suppose, but the reasoning was to an extent logical: make Inverness a less comfortable, less pleasant place to be, so that life became centred on True Home. What could be less pleasant, after all, than a camper van?

Try a camper van parked in the BBC's tarmac yard. Try a fifteen-year-old Italian camper van, left-hand drive, a coach-built Fiat with severe rust problems and an inside so dark and fusty you could have grown mushrooms. Commercially. Try moving in to this bizarre mobile shelter in mid-January – the coldest January for a decade.

I found the Fiat in Cullen, halfway between Inverness and Aberdeen (coincidentally, just five miles from Buckie, where I would buy the Trophy Olympic Gold). It was owned by a local mechanic, which I thought, foolishly, was a good sign. He told me its tale: an Italian tourist had brought it to Scotland, where he had fallen in love with a local woman and married. He had sold the camper, and the mechanic had bought it from him.

The Fiat had an expensive, coach-built Elnagh body, and came complete with an electric water pump, fridge (which never worked), cooker and mains hook-up. It had four berths. It was just nasty enough to suit my purposes.

As I drove the camper back to Inverness (it cost, as everything seemed to do back then, £2,500) the exhaust fell off. I pulled into the BBC car park in a crescendo of engine noise. Smoke was pouring into the cab, as the motor sat between the two front seats. I switched it off, determined not to

INTERNAL COMBUSTION

move the thing again until it was time to set fire to it in a lonely quarry somewhere and claim the insurance.

Wrapped in a four-season sleeping-bag, I just about survived that winter. I had the exhaust repaired. Every fortnight I went for a drive to charge the battery and fill the on-board tank with water. The van had a strange, ceramic, full-flush toilet, and a waste tank with a wide-nozzled drainpipe. I was dreading the day I would have to empty it, because of course there were times when that cludgie was the only WC available. I mean, stark naked in the Inverness BBC car park at 3 a.m., your options are limited.

Eventually, I decided to have a look at the sewage tank, and peered underneath in search of some kind of release valve. All I found was a bit of old string. I gave it a gentle tug. And a torrent of well-aged ordure and pee came fountaining out from under the Fiat onto the pristine surface of the car park.

The smell was indescribable. So I won't try to describe it. But it was bad.

Quickly, I released the string and moved the camper so that the large and spreading stain was largely disguised. The smell was another matter. I left for the pub, praying for rain and, thankfully, the heavens opened as I was downing Macallans and pints. On my return, all that was left of my accidental flushing were a few scraps of toilet paper and a vague scent reminiscent of Spanish holidays.

Eventually, I identified a few isolated lay-bys deep in the Highland forests where I could dump, so to speak, my load of shite. Every few weeks I would sneak off on my mission of second-generation defecation. I was the phantom shit-and-piss dumper of the Highlands, defiling tourist spots, taking revenge, on one occasion, on an infamous local pub for barring me. No, no details. But the Public Health Department had a field day with the contents of their cellar. The beer tasted funny for months, so I'm told.

In hindsight, it was probably a bad idea to take the family on holiday in the Fiat. I can't, for the life of me, remember exactly why we did it. Despite the building work on Shetland, there was plenty of money sloshing about at the time. Maybe it was just one of those let's-all-bond-in-an-unfeasibly-small-space sort of notions. But down flew *la famille*, and into the Fiat we crammed for visits to pals in Cromarty and, or so we intended, a trip to London to gaze wide-eyed at the glories of Oxford Street and the lost wonder that was Segaworld.

The thing is, no matter how much money you have, a hotel is hopeless for kids. There's all that stuff about not letting them run up and down the corridors letting off fire extinguishers, stopping noisy physical games and fraternal fighting, and that's without the problem of meals and mealtimes. Even those so-called 'child-friendly' hotels (always viciously expensive) have fixed tea-times in distant, hosed-down garages where your offspring can shovel fish-fingers and Chick Sticks down their gullets for exactly forty-five minutes before they are perforce locked in their rooms under the 'supervision' of a listening device monitored by a crack addict. So that their parents can put on smart clothes and pretend they're having a night out, eating crap food served by doped-up morons, drinking to numb the worry about the kids, only to have the dreaded Tannoy announcement call them to reception, where all three children have been locked in the luggage cupboard, having been found playing with plugged-in electric fires. In the swimming pool.

With a camper – or a caravan or indeed, if you have the built-in extremist masochism, a tent – you can get to a site, pitch the weans out into the ice and snow, let them exhaust themselves, feed them on Pot Noodles every ten minutes, and then send them to bed with Gameboys and Walkmans strapped on. Or something. Flexibility is the key. And, for that matter, cheapness.

So we headed for London. And got as far as Stirling. It was Easter, and the castle (one of the most underrated visitor attractions in, well, central Scotland) was packed. As I drove the low-slung Fiat into the car park, I ripped the exhaust system apart on a protruding kerb, unleashing a roaring noise so extreme that whole busloads of Dutch tourists stopped knocking back pints of yoghurt and gazed at us, open-mouthed, white stuff dripping onto the cobbles.

But when Susan stopped screaming, the noise from the broken pipe was still abysmal. And there was a problem. This Fiat was an Italy-only vehicle, the body was non-standard, and the exhaust was hardly what you would expect to find off-the-shelf in Kwik-Fit. Previous repairs had been complex.

I drove, nervously and noisily, to the Stirling Kwik-Fit Exhaust and Tyre Centre, expecting to be treated with the sneering boredom you tend to find in such places. But nothing could have been further from the truth. It was like a religious experience. A neatly overalled manager poked around under the camper, thankfully avoiding the string which opened the Floodgates of Shite and announced that the exhaust system had been welded and patched so often it was made up of about twelve separate sections.

'But don't worry,' he grinned, 'we'll sort something out.' And he did. With a hacksaw, an old exhaust system from a Ford Escort and some clamps, he put together a meandering arrangement of replacement pipework which sounded like the purring of a baby kitten. Well, acceptably eardrum-friendly, anyway. And he refused to take any payment. Kwik-Fit founder Tom Farmer being Scotland's best known and richest exhaust-pipe Catholic, I converted on the spot. Well, nearly. The Plymouth Brethren roots run a tad too deep for such mechanically orientated spiritual experiences.

Next day, we decided to visit the Blair Drummond Safari Park, where the Fiat broke down. Inside the lion enclosure. It's fair to say that there was a degree of tension within the van's increasingly sweaty confines as Simba the Rug padded about inches away, and I tried with increasing desperation to get the stalled engine to start.

'Daddy, will we be eaten?'

'No, no, we'll be on our way in a minute. Don't worry.'

'Daddy, can lions eat steel?'

'No, no, lions are vegetarians. Apart from eating meat, that is.'

'Daddy, can I open the window?'

'NO!'

After cooling for about ten minutes, the engine started again, but it was the beginning of a disastrous run of breakdowns which marred the rest of the trip. In Dundee the engine gave up the ghost on three separate occasions, and eventually the RAC's local agent (one of those independent recovery operators in a giant pick-up truck covered in STP stickers) diagnosed a faulty fuel pump (weird Italian type unavailable in Tayside) and we were ignominiously 'recovered' to Aberdeen on one of those enormous lorries with a car park on the back. The children didn't mind a bit. My wife hadn't spoken to me since the business with the lions, anyway, so another few hours made little difference.

In Aberdeen, a replacement fuel pump was found and the camper was again roadworthy. But, by that time, Susan and the bairns had flown home, and I was left to drive disconsolately back to Inverness, there to await the arrival of Chris Evans.

The episode which followed has been detailed in newspapers, TV programmes and at least one book, as crucial to the downfall to mere millionairedom of Evans, ginger-haired DJ-cum-vicious-blight-upon-cultured-humanity. He and his crew of sycophants decided it would be a jolly jape to broadcast his morning Radio One show from Inverness, at the same time as my own Radio Scotland effort came from the adjoining studio. The Evans team behaved like the ignorant, boorish bullies they sounded like on air, treating the women present, elderly BBC employees, any locals they came across and one local commercial radio DJ, the hapless Tich McCooey, as if they were shit on their shoes. Being at the time still an employed print hack with *The Daily Express* and *The Scotsman*, I took the opportunity to launch some mild missiles at the loathesome slimeball. I also revealed to the country just how badly behaved the Evans team was.

They were rattled. Matthew Bannister, then head of Radio One, asked BBC Scotland to shut me up. It was too late: the full wriggling-maggot

INTERNAL COMBUSTION

awfulness of the Evans phenomenon was in the process of being revealed. Soon he was out of Radio One and being patronising for England on Channel Four's *TFI Friday*.

Through this, I slept in the BBC car park, in my camper, wakened each morning by the Evans crew as they parked next to me, and left their shiny trails of sluggish gunge on the ground as they scraped themselves into the studios. Chris Evans came to Inverness, and retreated, wounded, but not, unfortunately, wounded enough.

After another six months, though, I was. The strain of the travelling began to tell. I started smoking again. On two occasions, I drunkenly slept in and had to be hauled out of the camper van by a producer. A producer who had to step gingerly over the pool of Macallan-flavoured vomit on the tarmac outside the camper van's door in order to wake me. One programme as I mentioned earlier was done entirely prone on the studio floor, a bucket handily positioned by my head. Another was slurred enough for even me to feel ashamed. Something was amiss. Me. I was turning into a parody of the egomaniac radio presenter, even more arrogant and opinionated than usual, but too fucked-up to deliver the goods properly. I was bored too, and would take stupid risks on air to make life more interesting. Like not scripting anything. Insulting guests. Going for long on-air pees during pre-recorded segments, leaving the shortest possible time to get back to the microphone, and just not caring.

It was time to stop. The house in Shetland now had the toilets (two, in fact) and an extension, the Birt-Hussey-Boyle-Cunningham Wing. And so I sold the camper van to a fireman and went home. Never again would I work like that, I swore. And no more camper vans. Absolutely not.

A month later I bought, from a retired pig farmer in Nairn, a 1977 VW Type Two, a basic camper, rusty, requiring work but essentially sound, I thought. I didn't tell Susan. Just brought it home on the boat after a quick trip away to satisfy the shockingly intense cravings for adrenaline brought on by not broadcasting anymore (a Radio Four commission to interview Tom Lehrer). My plan was to restore the camper to pristine, show-winning condition. Instead, I sold it to a birdwatcher for £200 less than I paid. He intended taking it to whatever twitching sites showed up on his computerised rare-bird-alarm pager, but frankly he would have been better just abandoning it somewhere perennially birdy, camouflaging it and using it as a hide. It was a swine of a thing. It smelt of rotting pork.

That should have been the end. But it wasn't. Somehow, I couldn't get the bug out of my system. The Last and Final Camper was another VW, bought to undertake yet another family holiday, now that we had no money left (tax, VAT and drug bills – drugs in the sense of stocking up my medical wife's pharmacy, I hasten to add). Last of the air-cooled Type Twos, this van was actually in good condition, came complete with a Caranex awning, which was supposed to open out the back end and give you double the internal space, and gave us reasonable service on a trip to London, even though the awning blew away at Crail during an ill-advised attempt to erect it in a gale. But we were all getting bigger, the adults in girth, the children in height, and without the awning it was basically far too cramped for comfort.

The end came in Edinburgh. I had been asked to present, for one night only, Scottish Television's Edinburgh Festival coverage, and we thought we'd make a family outing of it, taking the camper van to the Mortonhall caravan park (and crematorium, but that's optional) and letting the wife and kids roam Auld Reekie with money while I preened and pranced on the box.

All went well. I abandoned the Mortons and sold myself to TV, but I had a surprise in store. The budget included a hotel room for the presenter. And not just any old hotel room: a suite in the Balmoral, Sean

Connery's favourite hotel, which stands like a four-square security guard above Waverley station, lacking only the shaven head and tattoos. The room had a telly, video, fax, fresh fruit, a stunning view over Edinburgh, and a bed the size of a tennis court. You could comfortably have parked our camper van on one side of that bed.

I could have stayed there. But after the show had been broadcast, and I had sunk a few pints with the production team, I dutifully took a taxi back to the campsite, crawled into the VW over tightly packed, prone bodies, and draped what was left of a duvet over my shivering self.

I didn't sleep a wink. I lay there, cold, needing the toilet but unwilling to go wandering about outside looking for one, and thinking about that empty suite in the Balmoral. About a bed as big as the VW. About how I could have been there.

Two days later we took the VW back to Shetland and sold it to an elderly couple from Lerwick. They were remarkably short. We wished them well and took comfort in the fact that they would, unlike our expanding brood, have plenty of headroom. Oh, and they were thin as well.

Never again. Never again. Never again.

Now we have the Triumph Olympic Gold. It's far bigger than any of the campers. The Land Rover (highest towing capacity of any four-wheel drive, naturally) hauls it as if it weighs nothing, and it comes complete with an anti-shake device to avoid jack-knifing and other potential disasters.

No, it's not cool in the way that VW Type Twos are cool. It's about as groovy as knitted thermal underwear. But it's comfy. It's spacious. And the children love it. We can stay in London (well, Lea Valley) for £11 a night, all in, and there's a twelve-screen cinema next to the site. We can go anywhere. Move, stop, move on again.

And it has a great smell. It smells of my childhood, of a past where holidays throbbed with the excitement of impending, constant bliss. Maybe they weren't really like that, but for me the Trophy is a magic means of transport back there. True, now I have to take the responsibility, have the arguments with my own accompanying adult woman, not tip the thing over in an unfortunate U-turn accident. But I think I can cope. It doesn't have any gas lighting, but I have that Camping Gaz table lamp, and my Swan matches. And when the kids are asleep, and the butane is hissing, burning in a warm yellow light over my book, I'm at peace. I'm at home.

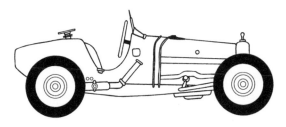

STRAP YOUR HANDS 'CROSS MY ENGINE

So you're mobile, then. So what? You can go to the shops, to work, on your holidays to Findochty. You can move from Partick to Charing Cross, from Swindon to St Ives, even from Caithness to Devon. But those aren't big trips, great, romantic, open-road adventures. Are they?

I did Scotland twice, both times for books and radio and, in one case, for telly as well. I thought I was some kind of bike-riding hero, though in both cases I tried to defuse the pose by including first a sidecar and a truly awful motorcycle, and for the second trip (for *Hell's Golfer*) the sure and certain lunacy of carrying a set of clubs on a large Kawasaki.

But Scotland isn't big enough. It certainly isn't sufficiently sizeable to support proper wide-scale pop-music-involving movement, travel or cars. Indeed, Britain's too small, a jaggy wee island criss-crossed by too busy, too narrow, too short roads. There's not enough room for serious movement. Too many obstacles. And the soundtrack's all wrong.

Think of something like Steppenwolf's 'Born to be Wild', that ultimate biker's anthem, linked forever to the sight of Peter Fonda and Dennis Hopper grooving down the long, straight highways of America on their choppers. Forget the fact that their horrible bikes probably couldn't do more than about 50 mph without falling apart and couldn't corner to save themselves. It's that image of the endless, lonesome, lost, Hank Williams highway stretching out in front of you, empty but leading to some so far invisible destination which just reeks of potential. Anything might happen in America if you go far enough. Get your motor running, head out on the highway. But in the UK? Start up your Honda 50, wrap yourself up well in oilskin and Barbour, leather and Gore-Tex, and take the bypass round to the industrial estate, where you can cut onto the little B-road that twists and turns past the sewage plant on its way to the nature reserve and the trout farm . . .

Where's the music for that? Reps may slam the *DriveSounds 2000* CD into their Mondeo's boot-mounted autochanger, and thrill to the soft snarl of Bob Segar, Bon Jovi's nauseating warble or such forgotten dinosaurs as Foreigner and Journey, but that's all American. British car songs have always been tongue-in-cheek like Tom Robinson's 'Grey Cortina', crappy and dumb like Chris Spedding's 'Motorbikin'' (compare and contrast with the daft but magical sonic swagger of Montrose's epic 'Bad Motor Scooter'), or (and arguably the best of the British journey pop songs) the early Leo Sayer elopement saga 'Moonlighting', ('Her blue Morris van was parked in an alley . . . My friend Danny he did the respray . . . so we couldn't drive it all last week') so perfectly detailed in its capturing of tiny, dull lives made briefly heroic.

Smallness. Irony. Crappiness. These tend to be the hallmarks of British motorised pop. There are exceptions. The Tom Robinson Band's '2-4-6-8 Motorway' (clearly something of a car fetish there, at least in the early days) is a masterpiece of runaway escapist internally combusting rock, but it's an isolated phenomenon. While there have been great driving songs (The Clash's 'Rock the Casbah', some U2) there has been hardly anything about cars and motorbikes worth even the briefest listen. I mean, David Essex's *Silver Dream Racer* soundtrack? (Still the only recent British biker movie; the world is ready for another one, probably starring biker Ewan McGregor and preferably watchable.) Primal Scream's 'Vanishing Point' just about does it, but those boys are infused with American blood, despite their Glaswegian antecedents. And *Vanishing Point* is of course an American (and not very good) transcontinental car movie. Good ending, though.

America. From 'Leader of the Pack' (for which the producer, my father's namesake George 'Shadow' Morton, took a Harley Davidson up in the lift of a Hollywood hotel in order to record the exhaust note in one of the bedrooms) along with the endless chug-a-lug travelling songs of country and blues, to Chuck Berry ('Maybelline' et al) through the directly descended Beach Boys Californian canon (Little Deuce Coupe, Little Honda) and onwards to the literate wanderings of Neil Young ('Woodstock'), Bob Dylan (any number of songs) and the whole phenomenon of highway rock, the music is about space, distance, the possibility of change. Movement.

And the names of the cars, too! Bob Dylan writes 'From a Buick Six', while Billy Bragg takes the piss with 'From a Vauxhall Velox'. You can write whole concept albums about Oldsmobiles, Cadillacs, Chevrolets and Mustangs (and my favourite, Mercuries, as in the stunning 'Mercury Blues') but you can hardly do that with Morris Minors, Hillmans or even Rovers and Jaguars. Crazy 'bout a Lanchester? I think not.

Yes, I know that a lot of this, in American terms, is about sex and money ('Every Woman I Know Is Crazy 'Bout An Automobile') and the phallic symbolism of something like a Chevrolet Corvette Stingray's bulbous penile bonnet is inescapable. But the notion of travel and escape is ubiquitous in American music.

The Bluetones, in 'Autophilia', not uncharacteristically, visited the great rock and blues tradition of 'Crazy 'Bout A Mercury' and Queen's catastrophic 'I'm In Love With My Car'. 'Autophilia' is full of rather twee versions of classic 'Pull Up To The Bumper' sexual innuendo. 'Allo John, gotta new motor? Cor, that's a big one! Lor luvva duck. Or as Ray Davies from the Kinks once said, 'Go steady on my clutch, go easy on the hills, and you'll get a lotta mileage outta me.' Best of all is Jonathan Richman's Roadrunner, which cleverly deconstructs the thumping road anthem into something self-consciously daft. It's like Springsteen for riders of Solex mopeds. But only listen to the slower version. Richard Thompson's majestic '1952 Vincent Black Lightening', as well as 'MGB GT', must also be mentioned.

And not just music. Literature is awash with petrol, and nowhere more so than in Raymond Carver: clearly, from the poems, a motor man to his oily fingernails. (How I love the poem 'The Car': 'The car waiting on the back lot/ Car of my dreams/ My car') But Carver also recognises the possibility of distance and movement in the vast American landscape as an engine for personal transformation, or at least providing a context for acting out what may prove to be an illusion. Like the man in one story who leaves his wife and children and vanishes, determined to change his life utterly, only to be found on the other side of the country, married with children, under a different name, working at the same job, living the same life with different people, in another place.

Springsteen is the man for mythologising American transportation. If Carver skewers the lie, Bruce (or the young Bruce) celebrates the hope that maybe, just maybe, it's true. Up to a point. Yes, there's the joyous orgasmic shout of 'Born to Run', where couples drive to the sea 'to wash these sins off our hands'; but there's also his early masterpiece, 'Darkness on the Edge of Town', where all roads lead to existential horrors too awful to mention in anything but the most biblical of language ('Tell her there's a spot out 'neath Abram's Bridge / And tell her, there's a darkness on the edge of town'). The album closes with the awful, bittersweet despair of 'Racing in the Streets', where life is reduced to the glorious, deadly meaninglessness of racing for money in illegal, edge-of-town meetings. Inspired by the film *Two Lane Black Top*, the song, like many of Springsteen's, is a soundtrack to a missing movie.

But for every 'Cadillac Ranch' there's a 'Pink Cadillac', for every 'Hungry Heart' there's a 'Thunder Road'. Until you get into the later Springsteen, where desperation sets into monotonous, sometimes unlistenable, effect. I mean, does anybody actually like the acoustic albums? Still, 'Mister State Trooper' from *Nebraska* (that cover says it all about distance, roads, travel) has been covered brilliantly by Johnny Cash, and that plea ('please don't stop me') echoes down the highways of Iowa and Nevada with a poignant whine. In Ayrshire or Chiswick, in Sutherland or Sunderland, it communicates a kind of hope and despair which we British cannot begin to grasp. And yet we long for it, we lust after it. Hence the British obsession with Americana, with bloody line dancing, country music. Even this insane bourgeois male desire to own a Harley Davidson, the most useless motorbike imaginable for British roads. Strap your hands 'cross my engines. Baby. I was born to be wild. Gotta Move. Get out of Denver Baby Go. Where, Abraham asked God, should Isaac should be killed? Dylan wrote: 'God said: Do it down on Highway 61.' Not the A66 near Penrith.

The only really big road trip I've ever undertaken happened during my first time in America, and it was a bizarre, three-week escapade, supposedly to write about a very unusual American tour by the Scots band Del Amitri.

This was Del Amitri Mark One, the slightly fey, angular, acousticky merchants of left-field pop, inspired by the likes of Wire and Television. Justin Currie, the lead singer, had not yet grown sideburns and affected leather jackets. He and Ian Harvie still had short spiky hair and wrote short spiky songs.

Justin and Ian later declared unilateral independence from the band as I knew it (Paul Tyagi on drums, Brian Tolland on guitar) and formed Del Amitri as it is now known and somewhat loved: sweet, dynamic power pop with an American rock edge and interesting lyrics. They have recruited new members and seem successful and happy. When I was travelling with them, they were neither.

The Dels had just been dropped by their record company, Chrysalis, and had decided to play America under their own steam, with a little help from their fans. I was amazed that they had American fans, but they did, and the idea was that this network of support would arrange gigs, coast to coast, put the band up in their houses and allow Del Amitri an insight into the Real America, man. Also, there was a hope that they would make a modicum of cash and possibly attract the attention of a record company.

I was going to write about the trip for *Melody Maker* and make a radio documentary for the BBC. So, with the band already in New York, I caught a North West flight out of Prestwick one July day in 1986. I would, I was assured, be met at Kennedy Airport.

I wasn't. Instead, there was a note at the information desk saying that I should get the subway into the city and rendezvous with the band on the east side of Washington Square. One giant lump of nervous trepidation, I made my way into the Big Apple.

No Dels appeared in Washington Square, not for four hours. In the end, I managed to contact one of the attendant girlfriends (Brian's; Fiona), on the only phone number I had for them, at a fan's house somewhere in New Jersey. From the tension in her voice, I could tell things were not going well. Somehow, I fumbled my way onto a bus at the Port Authority station and met up with Fiona in a particularly unappetising part of Jersey City. It looked like a bombsite. The only remaining tenement building was where the band (plus female manager Barbara, Paul's girlfriend/Ian's sister Lynne, old pal and support Kevin McDermott, and Fiona) were squatting with rabid fan Neil.

That night, jet-lagged to hell, I helped the Dels load their gear into two rancid Fords, including, of all things, an ancient Capri, and play at a club in Brooklyn. About thirty people turned up. Then we had to do a runner as it turned out Neil, who had organised the whole thing, had lied to the club's management and told them it was his twenty-first birthday party. When they found out that tickets had been sold, they tried to confiscate the band's equipment, which led to all of us heaving it out of a fire door while Jan tried to distract some heavy Brooklynites. We ended up in Long Island, hiding from Neil, the club owners and some irate fans, in the house of yet another fan. Or, rather, his mother's nice bungalow.

Next day, I went into New York with Ian and we hired a gigantic Chevrolet van with three rows of seats. There was just enough room for the nine-strong tour party and the gear. I drove the huge automatic truck back out to Long Island, through clichéd New York streets with smoking manhole covers, and extras from Michael Jackson's video for *Thriller* wandering around.

There followed two weeks in hell. The band, it became clear very quickly, were in the throes of a major falling-out. Everyone, apart from his girlfriend, appeared to hate Paul Tyagi. There was very little money. The gigs, which after Brooklyn were in Orlando, Florida, Georgia, Texas and, er . . . Los Angeles, were poorly attended and made hardly any cash. My feet smelt very bad indeed. Attempts at busking were interesting, but not very lucrative. Kevin got off with a girl in Orlando, much to the aggressive disapproval of her boyfriend. We nearly got beaten up, or worse, by a gang of coked-up Cajuns in New Orleans. Or maybe I imagined that. Because I was so tired I was beginning to hallucinate things. I mean, surely we couldn't all have got so fed up with Paul Tyagi (drummers: why do they always live up to their reputations?) that, when he flounced off to sleep in some Texas woods one desperate night, we attempted to drive off without him next morning, stopped only by Gail threatening to throw herself in front of the van? That couldn't have happened.

But I've mostly blanked out the snarling fights and the horrendous silent tension in the van. I volunteered to drive as often as I could stay awake, and it's those massive distances I remember, rumbling along freeways through the Carolinas, passing giant Peterson trucks, hundreds of prefabricated houses being moved around America on the back of lorries, burger restaurants, filling stations with ice by the sackload, free in cool states, paid for in hot ones.

Music worked with it, too, strange country stations playing weird bluegrass, mad preachers and, once, as the sun set over the New Mexico desert, Tears For Fears playing 'Everybody Wants to Rule the World', a record which unaccountably made me want to cry. We travelled. We moved. We drove all night, all day, on Route 66, across the endless bridge into New Orleans. We felt America, measured it out beneath our wheels, watched those vast landscapes unroll before us, and began to understand what energised American music. I don't think it was any coincidence that after this pilgrimage (the band were there for six weeks; I abandoned them, exhausted, in Albuquerque), Justin and Ian, the motor of Del Amitri, Americanised their muse, and turned themselves into a kind of cross between John Cougar Mellencamp and the Beatles. It was the travelling which gave them that sense of space which now inhabits their music. Allowed them to drop the fiddly chord changes and make themselves into a sixteen-wheeler, not a bubble car.

In Athens, Georgia, I had arranged to meet REM, who were then less than massive, and was ferried about in Michael Stipe's yellow checker cab and Mike Mills's vintage Oldsmobile. I interviewed Stipe for *Melody Maker*, in his newly purchased vegetarian café. 'You're driving across America?' he drawled, gently. 'Hey, this isn't a country, man. This is a continent!'

In the midst of an artfully staged, very theatrical interview scenario, in walked two diminutive figures, both dressed up as Alice Cooper, complete with full make-up. They were never introduced, but I later found out that one of them was Natalie Merchant, from 10,000 Maniacs, and the other a very, very young River Phoenix. It was all a kind of joke to unnerve me and make Michael laugh. He didn't turn a hair. And in those days, he still had hair.

Athens, a liberal university town infested with a kind of Tennessee Williams weirdness but set right on the buckle of the Bible Belt, was infested with a plague of locusts, fittingly enough. We went to a party where two people arrived wearing boa constrictors. Overnight, the house two along from where we were staying was hit by lightning and burned down. None of us heard a thing.

Next evening, we drove though electrical storms of apocalyptic fury, with huge bolts of lightning arcing down on either side of the road. It was frightening in a totally elemental way.

'Jesus Christ.' said someone.

'Shut up!' replied an agitated Justin, his religious background surfacing. 'This is no time for swearing!'

We came across whole music scenes where bands could sell hundreds of thousands of albums in their particular corner of America, and never gain fame outside of it. I began to understand the notion of constant travelling which is part of all American art. How country bands could stay on tour all the time, never revisiting the same town for years. When I hopped on a cheap flight from Albuquerque (for which, to this day, I owe Kevin McDermott $100) to LA, I watched the endless deserts pass beneath me and thought of Gram Parsons, dead and burning. Of the big country. And of wanting to get home to a very small one.

The radio series was never made, though seven tapes still linger in my files somewhere. *Melody Maker*'s features editor revealed that he hated Del Amitri and wouldn't have anything about the band in the paper. He loved REM, though, so my Mills and Stipe interview made it to the front cover.

Since then I've been back to America several times, driven around it a lot, but never had that same sense of enormity. I've driven in Europe, been flown around Africa, and incessantly criss-crossed the UK. But that vastness, that lostness, was something I think you only experience once.

When you go to the place you've heard about in songs and watched on telly and the movie screen, and you open your eyes to scenes you've only ever seen second-hand, and suddenly they're all around you.

The invitation from South Africa offered space, uncertainty, danger, strangeness, a tempting vastness; a continent, not a country. I was scared to accept. It was impossible to accept. Or, in the end, to turn it down.

PART TWO

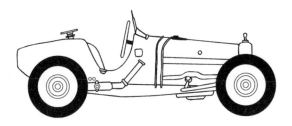

INTO AFRICA

t's a Nissan Sunny, no air-conditioning, and the radio says the temperature outside is thirty-five degrees. Just off a thirteen-hour flight from Amsterdam, I'm slouched in the passenger seat, bodily fluid rapidly evaporating. All I want to do is climb inside a giant refrigerator and sleep.

But that's impossible, given Cape Town's traffic conditions and my chauffeur's approach to driving. Rowan is an international hockey player and he wields his car like a stick. All the other drivers, though, are playing rugby with their vehicles, the full-contact, bone-crushing Afrikaans variety. Given a fraction of a chance those heavy, shaven-headed white guys in their bull-barred Toyota Landcruisers will snap wee Rowan's Nissan Sunny stick and shunt him into touch.

Somehow, we reach the freeway, where a police Opel Kadett zips by. I've heard the Johannesburg cops have been given a fleet of BMWs by BMW themselves, I inform Rowan, so concerned are the Bavarian firm by the stealability of their products and the associated muggings, deaths, injuries and general mayhem caused by carjackers. It's true, Rowan tells me, swerving around a packed minibus taxi, a Toyota. But the Opel's faster than the cheap BMWs the Jo'burg police have been given. It's not as if they've got M5s or anything. That Opel's a goer, he says. And anyway, far more Toyotas are stolen in South Africa than BMWs.

So, I gasp, my throat rapidly closing in the brain-melting heat, what are the arrangements for the trip? Rowan has been organising a voyage of semi-alcoholic discovery which will see me navigating myself from Cape Town to Johannesburg, taking in the new South Africa's brewing industry on the way. It's a commission for one of the clutch of new men's magazines currently cluttering the new South Africa's bookstalls; this one's for a local edition of *GQ*, and while the British version might look askance at drinkin'n'ridin', nobody cares about drink-driving in South Africa. In fact, it's seen as a bit of a macho achievement to be able to drive while you're incapable of walking.

To make the whole thing perfect from the commissioning editor's point of view, I should probably have sex with several models on the way, actually on top of the motorbike, at 100 mph, while pissed. I gather that it would suit the magazine were I to undergo several near-death experiences, and write the finished piece heroically in traction. I decide to make any sex stuff up, as my wife will ensure that I *am* in traction should anything like that really happen. And do my level best to avoid injury, as this will not meet with spousal approval either. I'd prefer not to get shot, either by my pump-action-armed significant other or by a Cape Town minibus taxi-driver. All of whom come complete with 9mm pistols.

'Oh, everything's coming together quite nicely,' says Rowan, screeching to a halt inches from yet another Toyota van full of people, and doubtless equipped with an AK47 or two. 'Got you a bike. The manufacturers were delighted to lend you it. Top of the range, too.'

I sense a hesitation in his voice, though it could just be the mini-roundabout he's driven over. 'What kind of bike is it, Rowan?' I'd originally been offered a Harley Davidson; I'd rather walk, I said, having experienced all the tractor-like, posing-accountant horror of a Harley on several previous occasions. If I walked, at least I'd have a chance of getting there. Everyone said the roads were good, but there was a Foreign Office warning on the Internet that British nationals should not drive on the N2 north of East London. This was part of my route, and I considered a Harley too stealable, too unreliable and too unwieldy for any potentially dodgy situation. South Africa had 'dodgy' written all over it, though as my friend Ingrid, long-time Jo'burg resident, put it: 'It could be worse, Tom. You might be going to Ghana. Or Sierra Leone.'

'It's a BMW,' Rowan replies, 'but don't worry, it's only BMW *cars* people like to steal. Not bikes. And anyway . . . '

'Toyotas are stolen more often,' I finish the sentence. 'But that's only because there are about ten times the number of Toyotas, Rowan.'

'Mugging,' muses Rowan. 'Worry about it too much and it'll happen, man. Don't think about it. Why worry?'

Well, I don't say it aloud, because it's safe to assume that all those muggers are armed, as you can pick up a Kalashnikov from the Terrorism Surplus Stores out in the townships for twenty-five rand, or three quid. Bullets extra, of course. Hence the weird and wonderful anti-theft devices to be found in South Africa, like flame-throwers mounted underneath cars so that attackers simply get barbecued. *Braai* (barbecues) being a crucial cultural phenomenon, as it were. And then there's guns. To quote Keanu Reeves in *The Matrix*, that philosopher in the most philosophical of films: 'Think lots and lots of guns'.

Big guns, wee guns, plastic guns, high-tech light-alloy guns. Machine-guns. One-shot guns disguised as pens. You name it, you can buy one in South Africa. They're advertised in women's magazines, for goodness' sake. This is why a very nice Belgian man called Jean has supplied me with a bulletproof vest for the trip, £300 worth of *Kevlar* and cotton which is good for 9mm Magnum pistol shells but, he stresses, 'will not stop AK47 and military rounds from rifle long distance'. So if a sniper wants me, I've had it.

If, that is, I'm wearing the bulletproof vest at the precise moment I get shot. As it happens, I'm not wearing it just now because (a) I would feel like an idiot, and (b) it's too bloody hot. Feeling like an idiot and being too bloody hot will pay a big part in this trip. Also (c) I'm vain and the vest makes me look as if I've been badly inflated. Like a Michelin Man in mufti.

According to the police statistics it is true that BMWs are beaten by Toyotas as the most popular targets for thieves. But there is a baleful silence when it comes to motorbikes. Are they a popular target for armed crims? And anyway, surely the point is that in a car, any car, you can lock the doors. On a bike, well. There you are, naked, so to speak. And in my case, with the bulletproof vest in one of my squashable bags, buried deep in Rowan's boot.

Suddenly, with a crash and the sound of rending metal, the aged Nissan merges itself with the back bumper of the pick-up truck, or *bakkie*, ahead of us. Five faces peer anxiously down at us from the flatbed. The driver hops out from the cab, just as Rowan throws open his door and confronts him. I think, Oh no, in South Africa twenty minutes and we're dead. I'm dead. Then it occurs to me: well, possibly only Rowan's dead. Don't shoot me, I'm only the passenger.

All the passengers and the driver of the *bakkie* are black. My fears are racist, no question, but the point is that in South Africa if you're white, the people with guns who are poor and want to rob you are black. And mostly they might as well shoot you, because a hell of a lot of whites have guns concealed about their persons and wouldn't think twice about shooting a black out of hand. Not only that, they're likely to get away with it too. I mean, I have sympathy with the poor blacks of South Africa but I sure as hell don't take it as far as the J.M. Coetzee I-feel-so-guilty-about-racism-you-might-as-well-rape-my-daughter-and-I'll-forgive-you-because-it's-your-right-to-be-a-bastard stance. Two wrongs, as they say, don't make a right. Sometimes clichés are kind of true. Which is why they're clichés. Like that statement.

Anyway, Rowan and the driver are talking, gesticulating and then . . . laughing and slapping each other on the back. There's some tugging of bent metal. Rowan gets back into the car and reverses clankily, accompanied by some metallic tearing noises. Then, with a snort of horns and waves, we are away.

'It was stolen,' Rowan tells me. 'Or borrowed, at least. The guy didn't seem bothered at all, and this thing's a pile of junk anyway. He was cool about the whole business. Happens all the time.'

Yeah, except most of the time you get shot, I want to add, but who am

I? Just another paranoid tourist. 'But . . . but weren't you worried? He might have been armed.'

'Naaah, man! This is Africa. You just got to go with it. What happens happens.'

What happens happens. I wondered how my specialised travel insurance, taken out at vast expense in London, would cope with such a philosophy. Knock for knock it wasn't.

'What about insurance for the bike?' I ask. 'Will BMW take care of that?'

A pause. 'Probably.' Rowan turns to look at me, thankfully only for a second, giving him time to swerve past a digger which is proceeding slowly down the inside lane. 'We're not big on insurance here. There's no legal requirement for third party cover. Or maybe there is but nobody has it. There's no point.'

'Fine,' I say. Fine. Just take me to a fridge and let me stick my head in it for a hour or two.

'Oh, well, we can't go to the hotel just yet,' says Rowan, 'you have to pick up the bike.'

Out of the grainy, brutal sun and into the rubbery air-conditioned dullness of the showroom, I am suddenly several thousand miles and thirty years away, and instead of standing in a BMW dealer in Belville, deep in the Boer suburbs of Cape Town, I am in Cooper Brothers at Templehill, Troon, Ayrshire, gazing with my pal Stewart Howard at a glittering green Triumph Trident, one of the last gasps, though we had no inkling of it then, of Britain's dying motorcycle industry. Lusting without hope, fantasising in silence, we were fourteen and had two years to go before we were even legally entitled to take to the road on two wheels. But Les Cooper was someone who thought long term, who never missed an opportunity to cultivate a potential customer. And so he hailed the two school-uniformed adolescents, took us into his office and regaled us with tales of the TT, his big crash, seeing his own leg stuck in a tree as the rest of him slid down the road with his crushed bike.

I shake such thoughts away, a forty-five-year-old man scared of death, amputation, injury, in fact most things hurtful to humanity, or my own personal piece of it. And motorbike-related injury is much on my mind. Along with shooting and mugging, seeing as the next ten days are to be spent riding a large lump of motorised German bicycle through South Africa, winner of the international Murder, Violence and Terrorising of Tourists Award for the last five years.

'The bike's outside.' The voice is gruff, Afrikaner and emanates from a bearded figure of considerable girth. I turn from the assorted quads, jet skis, Suzukis and BMWs of every shape and cost, from the heady aroma of tyres and petrol, burnt oil and cigar smoke – Les Cooper was the first person I ever met who smoked Hamlets, and from then on that choking reek spelt glamour and danger – and head out into the violent heat of a February Cape day.

I never bought a bike from Cooper's, which is long closed. Troon, too, is much changed, from the bourgeois golfing backwater in which I grew up to something much stranger; a schizophrenic community. There are the rich, the super-rich golfers (it's Royal Troon now, the championship course, not Old Troon) and yachtie types who cluster around the marina with its seafood restaurant, down where the shipbreakers' yard used to be. There are big houses and a school, Marr College, still acceptably middle-class in its accomplishments. But there is also a town centre now shabby and somehow shrunken, the pubs dismal and slightly threatening, the hotels draughty and badly painted, off-season smelling of dampness and half-staved-off decay.

A&D Frasers, the garage from which we bought petrol and sometimes cars, has vanished, but my first car did come from there, the MG which buried my dreams of leather-jacketed two-wheeled glory for nigh on fifteen years. But cars came after the dalliances with Cooper's: scooters, mopeds and the ferocious visceral thrill of biking. All wrapped up and safely cocooned within the steel and glass walls of a four-wheeled capsule by the age of seventeen and a half. Of course it couldn't last.

So I'm baking beneath an African sun (thirty-five degrees in the city bowl, they're saying) and the fat Afrikaner is asking me if I've ever ridden a R1150GS before, while I gaze at this immensely tall, inconceivably ugly pile of Bavarian plastic and metal in a very different way from the awed drooling that Stewart and I used to treat the green Triumph triple to. Because, in a matter of seconds, I know I'm going to have to climb aboard this monstrous semi-trail bike and ride it back into Cape Town, the first time I have ever driven anything on South African roads. Roads which, particularly in the case of Cape Town, I have been warned are awash with armed and casually dangerous minibus drivers (black). And psychotic, fascist semi-Afrikaners (whitish) who hate Brits. And Scots are Brits, in this context. Only the Irish are honorary Boers, as it is assumed that they hate the British too.

And I don't want to ride this bloody huge motorcycle into Cape Town. Still less do I fancy the couple of thousand meandering miles which lie between me and Johannesburg. I am forty-five, for God's sake! I have a family, responsibilities, a mild heart condition and piles! Afraid? I'm terrified!

But I'm even more petrified of crapping out of the agreement I've made with Daniel, editor of *GQ* South Africa, to ride this beast around his adopted land, sampling beers produced by the post-apartheid rash of new microbreweries. Under the previous regime, South African Breweries, producers of the dreaded Castle Lager (white) and Lion Lager (black), had a virtual monopoly on swillable ales.

By the way, you're not to mention colour at all in the new South Africa; not in newspaper reports, not in marketing. Which means that the drinks salespeople have a hell of a time spelling out what they're up to, as everything's labelled differently for the black and white consumers. Castle and Lion ('Lion means strength to the black man,' I am told by a white beer buff) and anything royal in the name of a whisky for black as opposed to the simple Bells and Black Label for whites.

INTERNAL COMBUSTION

117

'Ever ridden a BMW before?' The Afrikaner BMW man is eyeing me doubtfully as I pull on helmet, winter gloves, leather trousers, boots and Cordura jacket. I have seen several motorcyclists since arriving here, and they have all been dressed in shorts, T-shirts and flip-flops. I mutter a yes, having cut my second-time-around biking teeth on the R65LS, the sporty 650 which looks like a Suzuki Katana and goes like an arthritic warthog thanks to its ancient boxer engine. But this massive thing before me has a boxer-flat twin motor too, albeit a more advanced, computer-controlled thingummy. 'It will,' I announce loftily from within the depths of my Shoei helmet, 'be a piece of piss.'

Approximately twenty-six-and-a-half years after taking to the road on two motorised wheels for the first time, I am not on the biggest motorbike of my bi-wheeled riding career (a Harley Fat Boy is heavier, wider, uglier and has a heftier engine) but nearly, swerving through the suburban Capetonian traffic as big gusts of hot Indian Ocean wind come buffeting in like meteorological bullies.

Rowan is leading me through the traffic as if he's on some kind of mission from God to kill me. Perhaps he is, and Dan the editor has invited me here to have me die in some horridly hot road smash, in order to give him an exciting front cover for the next issue. But no. That's paranoia. That's ridiculous. I slither to a halt in a traffic jam, and nervously eye the drivers surrounding me for guns. Underarm bulges. Nothing visible. Lots of Mercedes, though, and BMWs. I'm naturally nervous, as you can probably tell. But nerves can work to your advantage, helping to keep you aware and, just possibly, alive. That's what I'm hoping, anyway. My leather trousers stick to the seat, and my thighs adhere, viciously and hair-trappingly, to the trousers. There's two thousand miles of this to go. Occasional fevered, panicky glimpses upwards show Table Mountain, awesome as ever, but I need to keep my eyes glued to Rowan's battered Nissan if I'm to make it to the hotel. There's the Newlands rugby stadium on the right . . . last time I was here, I watched Ireland get gubbed into the winter mud. Any mud has long since turned to cement.

The line of cars suddenly screeches to a solid static mass in front of me, so I slam on the brakes. ABS? On a bike that means the brakes judder on and off with the alarming, not to say terrifying, sensation that they've simply stopped working. Somehow, I come to a halt centimetres from Rowan's back bumper. Breathing heavily into my helmet, I wonder what on earth I'm doing here, decrepit, married with oodles of children, risking my neck for . . . what? Money? I'm being paid, but no more than I could have earned in the UK without placing my bottom astride a massive bike for days on end, in a strange and potentially lethal country. Prestige? The article will be published in a South African magazine only. The thrill? Actually, I'm terrified. So scared I've made a will, written last letters to my family and bought that bulletproof vest I don't dare tell anyone about.

No. I'm here because I can't stop. Because journeying, moving, travelling is built into my bones. Because the idea of a road trip sends all kinds of chemicals coursing around my bloodstream, and movement, I know, calms me. I'm like a baby who needs the rocking movement of his mother's arms and, as Bruce Chatwin argues in *The Songlines*, maybe that's a throwback to the days of wandering tribes, to the sense of comfort in moving, always moving. It's what I do. Who I am.

That's what I tell my wife, and it never sounds like anything other than pompous, preening, macho bullshit. Or so she tells me.

In the hotel's underground car park, I switch off the GS's engine and sit for a moment listening to the catalyser crackle and ping as it cools down. It is as I suspected. It is a typical BMW. Beautifully made, solid as a rock and easy to ride apart from the hellish gear-change. I have kick-started old BSAs easier than finding first from neutral on this huge yellow creature with its prehistoric, horribly recalcitrant transmission. Its shaft drive, though, is like every BMW except the little F650, which is made in Italy and not really a BMW at all. So no breaking chains, just that weird torque-roll, that twist beneath you when you gun the throttle.

Half falling, half stumbling off the bike, I gradually peel off my various items of protective clothing. With them comes what seems like half a stone's worth of liquified fat, particularly evil-smelling sweat, containing no doubt the disgusting KLM airline food I suffered the previous night. I sway from side to side, pile up my various bits and pieces and head for the air-conditioned comfort of my room. I haven't even started the trip yet. Only two thousand miles to go.

I can wait.

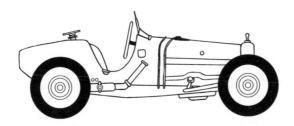

TWO PINTS OF LAGER AND A PACKET OF CRISPS PLEASE

For now, though, I'm naked beneath the air-conditioner, and I'm thinking beer. Here's the plan in all its ineffable, self-indulgent stupidity and glorious wonder: South Africa is rediscovering beer in its non-Castellated, properly brewed, interesting and tasty sense. People are sick of oral anaesthetic through chilled South African Breweries products, and want something more. Forget the fact that home-brewed *sorghum* (maize beer) has been available forever in the black community. That's black. And though it's never said, my job is to report in a white way, for whites and for blacks who wish they were white or think they are. It is my task to unearth some of these newly minted ales, lagers, stouts and, well, beers, and . . . drink them.

On a motorbike, you ask, incredulously. What about road safety? Well, one hand on the handlebars at all times . . . Or more to the point, taxis when unable to stand. Maybe I should have had a sidecar attached to the GS. Drink and driving, or riding, do not mix, he said sternly and with an enormous exhalation of moral righteousness and fervour. It is bad, it is wrong, it is dangerous, you could kill yourself and dozens of other people.

And yet, and yet . . . how many of us have a perfect history of non-alcoholic road use? Who hasn't risked that last half pint (hey, three and a half pints of lager over four hours, and you lose half a pint's worth of alcohol every hour, so that's . . . probably okay then)? Who amongst us doesn't thank God or our lucky stars or watered-down whisky for that wavering, weaving trip home, grossly ill-advised after a night's benderdom?

Some shameful and inexcusable examples:

(1) The Islay Hotel car park, during the filming of the TV series *Spirit of Adventure* based on my book of the same name.

(2) Driving back through Clarkston on the southern outskirts of Glasgow, two bottles of Lambrusco and a couple of cans to the wind, in a Honda Civic, with my sullen but cool (or sullenly cool) girlfriend beside me, about 2 a.m. after a party at a workmate's house. I mean, Lambrusco. Well, Lambrusco with Superlager chasers. Serious, stupid drinking.

Mee-maw, flashing blue lights, flashing headlights. Over I pull, wind down the window, try to talk while breathing in and without slurring my words . . . but the face staring in at me is Bobby, drummer in my part-time rock'n'roll band and most un-pc PC, and he grins as he asks to see my licence, then waves me on my way without a hint of recognition. He didn't let his colleague have a sniff, for which I shall be forever grateful. He may be a chief constable somewhere now for all I know. He was a great drummer. Having partially sobered up due to an adrenaline overload, I made it home without incident. I can't remember if the sullen girlfriend and I managed to achieve sexual congress or not . . . Lambrusco and Superlager, it seems certain, cannot be conducive to top-rated sexual performance.

(3) Desperate nights among the Glaswegian *demi-monde* in the early 1980s . . . oh yes, the tales I could tell of violence, drugs, adultery and having to leave town in a hurry. But, no, I will confine myself to the time I was so drunk I couldn't speak, at a club called Fury Mury's, deep in the armpit of the old city. Instead of speaking, I just threw drinks at people and was sick over my instantly ex-girlfriend (not the sullen cool one; this one was just sullen). Woke up in my own bed, way up in the northernmost Brooksides of Glesca, with all the doors in the house open, and a car engine running somewhere near by. Staggering to the door, I saw my MG

Maestro – parked on the lawn, front driver's door open, engine and lights still on. Fortunately it was the kind of neighbourhood where they didn't call the police. About anything. Frank McAvennie used to live next door.

(4) Stopped by police at a roadblock just outside my housing estate (they were looking for an escaped prisoner; it was Summerston, for goodness' sake!), I took advantage of the queuing traffic to try, in an inebriated haze, a trick I'd been told disguised any scent of booze on one's breath. Sucking a copper coin, it seemed, did the business in this aromatic regard. What the hell, I thought, why not a few copper coins? And so I crammed my mouth with one- and two-pence pieces, and sucked the filth of millions of fingers off them.

Unfortunately, I forgot to remove them until it was too late, and when the policeman asked me if I had, perchance, unknowingly concealed an escaped murderer in my luggage area, I spluttered about fifty pence in loose change onto the roadway. He was so amused he let me go away, unimpeded, and slightly poorer.

Spirit of Adventure was a book about my motorcycle journey around Scotland's malt whisky distilleries. Somehow I survived, and then Scottish TV came up with the bright idea of making a TV series which involved repeating the entire trip, this time with a film crew in tow. To meet health and safety obligations, most of the filming was done with the bike on a low-loader, towed safely behind a Suzuki mini-jeep which burnt out four clutches in the course of filming. This time we took along an extra-large white van to contain all the free samples of booze which, believe me, proved necessary. The van and the booze.

So everything was fine. We had six weeks of travelling, eating, boozing, golfing and filming, all expenses paid, and I only had to ride the MZ occasionally, and then when it was securely attached to the low-loader. Except that, naturally, we sometimes got bored of an evening, far from home, and decided to make our own entertainment. Like on Islay.

Here's a thing: the BBC had all but taken over the hotel when we arrived, as they were filming, at vast expense, the new version of *The Vital Spark*, with Gregor Fisher, Rikki Fulton and others. And things were going very,

INTERNAL COMBUSTION

very badly indeed. They had built a set in the wrong place, so it couldn't be used. The puffers out in the Sound of Jura kept breaking down or going adrift. The weather was atrocious. And then we turned up, having a great time, and on overtime rates which made the poverty-stricken Beebsters apoplectic with rage when we bought them all drinks in the bar. To be blunt, there was a fight. Or a bit of a scuffle. Media folk, when they get together, they're like kids, or worse, and as our STV guy came off slightly worse in this confrontation, we decided to get our own back.

So we appropriated – some might say stole – one of the walkie-talkies the BBC were using to direct marine operations during their very complicated filming of the two puffers pretending to be Para Handy's *Vital Spark*. And as the Beeb made desperate attempts to make up for lost time, we spent the whole day barking disinformation over the airwaves, and watching the result through binoculars.

'It's sinking! Abandon ship immediately! Dangerous killer whale sighted . . . divers in water beware!' That sort of thing. Apparently the only thing which gave us away was my stupid assertion that a nuclear submarine was heading for Port Ellen, and that activity should be halted. They checked with the Holy Loch and were told that no submarines were active in the area.

But to the car park! Now it can be revealed. In the hotel yard were parked two dozen vintage cars for the BBC shoot, beautifully preserved and very valuable pieces of motoring history – ancient Rileys, Wolseleys and even a Rolls-Royce. We had fallen in with two truly disreputable motorcycle journalists who were test-cruising a Honda Goldwing and a Harley Tourglide on the island, and we decided to have a little race.

It was one o'clock on a Sabbath morn, we had a tray of whiskies and a couple of bottles of Lagavulin we'd been given, and we decided to do time trials around the car park using the MZ. And the Harley. And the Honda. For two hours, we slid and sprayed gravel everywhere, oblivious to any damage we might cause, and for some reason we were ignored by everyone. Perhaps because, indoors, everyone else was blind comatose pissed.

Next morning, several of the valuable vintage and veteran vehicles were pitted and scarred. Or, at least, they were the night before by torchlight, so presumably they were worse under the watery Hebridean sun. We weren't there to see for ourselves. Clutching our hangovers like cancers, we had slipped onto the early ferry back to West Loch Tarbert, like drunken, stupid criminals.

First things first. Clothes, but this is South Africa, so not very many. And then out into the city for a bit of drinking. Sorry, I mean research. If we're talking beer in Cape Town, we have to be murmuring 'Mitchell's', even if the Waterfront microbrewery and its attached Scottish Ale House is a gentrified, kitsch outpost of the main operation in Knysna.

But the Mitchell's operation has come a long way since Lex Mitchell began hubbling and bubbling his hops and yeast in Knysna way back in 1983. Now there is a brewery in Gauteng, and the whole company has been owned by the UK's largest brewing concern, Scottish & Newcastle, since 1998. It's S&N's toehold in the South African marketplace, and probably the beginning of a major push into bar ownership, distribution and brewing.

Holy Saltires! I walk into Mitchell's as the sun fades over the mountain and I'm in someone's nightmare vision of a Scottish pub. Let me tell those of you who don't happen to live in Scotland about the Scottish pub. First of all, there have to be torn leatherette seats, encrusted with ancient vomit. A couple of elderly people of indeterminate sex asleep on the floor, along with four Jack Russell terriers. Something, allegedly beer, called Tennent's or McEwan's on sale, and an aggressive, shaven-headed, ex-army psychopath in the corner muttering, 'You lookin' at me, pal?' every so often and splintering a large piece of the wall with his forehead every five or six minutes.

Just like the Scottish Ale House, in fact. No, I'm only joking. The barmaid has the expression of a glum herring, but she claims this is due to having just been to the dentist. I order a Castle for me and some oil of cloves for her.

In South Africa, the problem is not whether you drink and drive, but what you might do if you are drunk and driving. You might, for example, pull out your hidden .38 and shoot the innocent, if reckless, bastard, who's just cut you up at a roundabout. You might collide with somebody's brand new Range Rover and get shot for your pains. You might pile into one of the many pedestrians tramping down the road, oblivious to traffic. The police have so much to do picking up the pieces after muggings, shootings, murders, rapes and pile-ups that breath-testing is very low on their lists of priorities – although they do it, occasionally.

My favourite drink-driving story ever, anywhere, concerns a South African journalist (it would be a hack) who had been knocking back Castles by the dozen down on the Eastern Cape, and was merrily, and very erratically, driving homewards when he spotted a police roadblock ahead. With lightning-fast reactions so admirable it's hard to believe he was actually pissed, he put his foot to the floor and ducked down beneath the dashboard, heading straight for the wooden roadblock. Having smashed right through, he popped his head up again and drove at top speed for a couple of miles before sliding the car to a stop, jumping out, opening the boot, leaping into the boot and slamming the lid behind him. Soon the sound of sirens signalled the arrival of the cops, and the heroic journo began banging on the inside of the boot-lid, screaming for help. When the police eventually opened the boot, he stared up at them in grateful love and affection: 'Thank God!' he sobbed. 'I thought I was a goner for sure! Those bastards had guns, man, and they forced me to get into the boot before they drove off . . . I was sure they were going to kill me!' Supposedly, he got off scot free.

As this only works in a context where carjackings at gunpoint are commonplace, I would not advise you try it in the UK. However, feel free to attempt it if you happen to be facing a similar situation in a foreign clime where the crime rate is high, and you are capable of thought processes as quick as the hero of this tale. I doubt you will be.

It might work in Northern Ireland, come to think of it.

I should say that I disapprove of drink-driving, on the whole. Unless, say, on a hard-packed beach after midnight, when all donkeys, stray dogs and seals have gone to bed, and you can perpetrate skid turns to your heart's content. Barassie, at the Troon side, used to be perfect for this. Switch the lights off and, harming no one, behave like an absolute pillock. Drive into the sea, stall the car, wade out and go home, returning sober to find it covered by the advancing tide. Hey, that's what I call a good night!

Impossible to be anything but scathing now, at my advanced age. But this is now, and then I was stupid, irresponsible and . . . lucky.

Mitchell's is heating up, guys hopping off Harleys just outside the door, wandering in, their white knees gleaming in the ultra-violet. *Caaauuustle*, they say. Castle. Castle. They clump down their tiny, semi-pushbike helmets and glance lovingly out at their gigantic two-wheeled tractors. I hate Harleys.

Castle Lager. It's yellowish, it's cold, it's bubbly and it tastes of . . . nothing much. Castle for whites, Lion for blacks. I can't get over this. It's insane. But huge amounts of cash are ploughed by major companies into separate marketing divisions for the black and white communities. It's like the old race industries of North America, where all kinds of products were specifically targeted at what was, in all senses, a black subculture. I once heard a drunk Afrikaner perfumier, of all things, waxing lyrical about how 'blacks prefer perfumes which smell of woodsmoke and cooking; it's a tribal thing'.

Anyway, Castle is an industrial beer, brewed over-strength and then diluted down with carbonated water. Nevertheless, it hits a (if not *the*) spot. And this is the problem, because generations of South Africans have been reared on Castle or its indistinguishable stable-mate Lion and, it does do the business. It quenches, and in sufficient quantity, it wrenches you all out of shape. It's got enough bitterness to be moreish, but not enough to tingle the palate. It's fizzy, but not so bubbly you're going to expand into the shape of an inflated Sumo until someone sticks their little prick in and you, uh, deflate embarrassingly. It works. It's better than Tennent's or McEwen's. It doesn't taste of rancid aluminium. And it's cheap.

The glum-faced barmaid makes me what she calls a 'ploughman's tea' out of cheese, pickles and clove-scented tears. The ploughman's lunch was invented in the 1930s at English roadside pubs, one of the first ersatz rural idylls on a plate. I long for vinegar-and-grease newspaper, the exultant expectation of burning chips against the palate. But no. It's slimy dill pickles and odd slippery cheese. The ploughman's tea is definitely a Capetonian speciality.

Eating has always been for me one of the great pleasures of travelling. The gradual building of hunger as the miles pass, and then the delights, or otherwise, of a restaurant, café, pub or carry-out. It is elemental satisfaction. Movement, sustenance and, then, if you're very fortunate, great toilets in which to have a different kind of movement. Such a combination can be very hard indeed to find.

Childhood Saturday and Sunday drives out of Glasgow usually involved a hotel north of the city called the Bailie Nicol Jarvie, a character from Sir Walter Scott's *Rob Roy*. Imprinted in my mind is the aroma of cigars and cabbage, bent wood furniture, sticky carpets and, somehow, dangerous, glamorous romance. 'Let's go to the Bailie Nicol Jarvie,' Dad

Me in a cowboy
hat, aged six.

Father and son,
with the Sprite
Major and Ford
Zodiac.

So cool: the Fiat 500
before the accident.

The romance of motorcycling: heading off on the glorious Orange Beast to research *Spirit of Adventure*. (Picture: Mick Murphy)

Mum, sisters, me and a Hillman Super Minx Estate with hired caravan. The caravan's handbrake was left on accidentally for the whole holiday, burning out the clutch.

If only it had always been this way:
the camper van at Scourie, 1988.

Paddy and Mrs Carolan in the annexe to their bedroom. Seriously. 'We may have been the polecats of the world, but they still bought our shit!'

The BMW outside the Birkenhead Brewery. It was hot.

From a safe distance, it was hypnotically attractive: bush fire near Stanford.

End of the road: ready to leave South Africa with unidentified cold sore/insect bite. My new TV contract stipulated that I should 'not have suffered from cold sores for a period of four months prior to filming.'

Near St Tropez for the launch of the Honda S2000, with cameraman John Agnew in typical Francis Ford Coppola pose.

Launch of the Nissan Primera in the Vosges Mountains near Strasburg. The *Wheelnuts* crew see trees for the first time.

The BMW that wasn't quite as well-preserved as it looked, at the Eshaness Lighthouse, Shetland.

Two Toyotas at rest: Susan's Hi-Lux and the unbelievably tedious Carina CDX.

Citing the Bruce Willis precedent: filming *Scottish Passport* in Oban with the Triumph Tiger.

would say, and something would leap within me, as a five-year-old. Or there would be drives out to the old Renfrew Airport which had a 'Milk Machine'. Iced milk or, better, orange juice, rumbling and tumbling from the depths of the big blue-and-white edifice when you put in the huge sum of six old pence.

Or picnics. Stopping the car (the Wolseley, maybe the VW) during some Highland jaunt with friends. Spreading tartan travel rugs. Into the weird, silent, silver jungle of the forest looking for a stream to get water for tea. The smell of methylated spirits as the stove was assembled and lit. The magic of hot tea by the side of the road. Cold sausage rolls. Wagon Wheels. Then moving on, moving on, moving on.

Best of all, though, chips, coming back to Glasgow or Troon from visiting the grandmothers in Bellshill, which was then, in the early '60s, still at the epicentre of Lanarkshire's great belching, smelting, smouldering range of heavy industries. Pit bings soared in the daytime, and by night, amid the choking, acrid smells of fire and brimstone, we drove, not past, but right through Colville's Ironworks, where molten metal sparked and showered and flowed, and we kids cowered terrified on the floor of the car, waiting . . .

For chips. Going back to Ayrshire, we would veer, somehow, from Cambuslang to Strathaven, where Dad would get out and come back later clutching a huge, newspaper wrapped parcel, steaming, fragrant with grease, salt, fish, vinegar. Somehow, no matter how much we ate, we were still hungry.

And we ate while moving, the heat from the food gradually seeping deliciously through paper onto knees, into laps. The engine roaring from gear to gear, a bottle of Barr's Irn Bru passed from mouth to mouth, shared grease on the neck, learning to let the air in as you raised it and drank. And still the darkness, made blacker by occasional house and street lights flickering by, then howling, grunting as the windows were opened, and the balled-up chip papers were chucked out, heedless of litter, when the dead smell of old fish suppers began to hang cold and heavy among us.

Until, comforted by fat, we curled up and slept, all of us, Mum included, as Dad alone stared out through the windscreen into the rushing onwards.

'Hey, you're from Scotland?'

I hesitate to admit it in this compendium of fake Caledonian chiclessness. Scotch Ale House, indeed. But the talk is sportive. Celtic have been beaten by no-hope second-division side Inverness Caledonian Thistle in the Cup. Have I seen the headline in *The Sun*? 'Super Caley Go Ballistic, Celtic Are Atrocious'? Yep. Best journalism since Sidney Schamberg wrote *The Killing Fields*. I order Mitchell's own lager, Forrester's Draught. Suddenly I'm in Czechoslovakia. Or the Czech Republic, these days. Wow, this is good. Light, not too harsh, but with much more of a hoppy edge than Castle. Tangy. Fragrant.

Time for a piss.

The toilets in Mitchell's are amazing. There are huge tanks, all copper and bound wood, great lengths of tubing, and the smell of spent beer everywhere.

It's only when I spy the piled sacks of unidentified grain that I realise I'm pissing in the brewery. God Almighty, what is this toilet bowl? Thought it was a bit big. How much have I had? Quickly, I zip up and make my escape, wondering if it's the lager or the bitter I've contributed to. Thank God I'm not driving. Or riding.

Back in the bar, I sample the Bosun's Bitter, which is okay, like a pale ale, but not heavy enough for my tastes. I'm probably too shocked by my accidental lavatory avoidance to assess the stuff properly, and, besides, my sinuses are acting up. Time for bed, unmugged, unraped, unthreatened, here in the crime-ridden Republic of South Africa. It isn't like this in Glasgow. In Glasgow I'd be in hospital or I'd know I hadn't had a good night.

Daniel the editor drives me back to the hotel in his leather-seated Honda Civic GT something or other. 'I love this country,' he says. 'There are no rules. No cameras to watch you when you're driving, or out on the streets. No regulations to tie you down. That's the Hard Rock Café which was bombed, by the way . . . ' he laughs. 'Hey! One night in Cape Town, and you haven't been mugged, raped, shot or killed. Aren't you disappointed?'

I laugh. Absurdities come up often in South Africa. The trick is to realise they exist. And take the piss. Always take the piss.

Next day, I'm to head out towards Stellenbosch, the wines of which I have sampled to excess on several occasions, partly because I was once paid for a job I did in South Africa in the form of twelve cases of best Stellenboschian stuff.

Unfortunately, it cost me fifty quid a case in customs duty and excess freight when it eventually got to the UK. But hey, who cares about cash after three bottles?

This time, I've got the money upfront.

Early, very early next day, I pack the BMW's custom panniers and head for Stellenbosch. In South Africa, the mostly two-lane roads have wide hard shoulders you're meant to pull over into, while maintaining your speed, if faster traffic comes up behind you. It takes a little while to master this. And to learn the trick of flashing my hazard warning lights in thanks when someone gets out of my way. I learn, though, as the morning heat rises inexorably, and I thank God I'm not wearing my bulletproof vest. The countryside is kempt, controlled and intensively farmed, and the idea of civil unrest seems bizarre. Until you spot the pedestrians, universally black, trailing along the road, or crammed seven or eight to a *bakkie*, and gazing into nothing and nowhere. This is white country, still, rich and controlled.

Stellenbosch itself is hotter than hell by the time I get there, and full of students, just like the real hell. It reminds me of Nashville, but without Dolly Parton and steel guitars. There are a lot of Harleys and student-type jeeps; this is not a poor college town. There is the smell of loose cash in the air.

Up a stair in one of the town centre malls is Tollie's, only just reopened under new ownership, and a brew-pub in the classic, barrel-lined mould.

Boykie De Klerk was a brewmaster at the giant South African Breweries for fifteen years, working on the whole range of that government-linked company's products, from *sorghum* to lagers. Latterly, he was a training officer for would-be brewers, and now he sets up microbreweries throughout the country. Tollie's, though, is his baby, and the week-old Tollie's Draught (just 5.5 rand a pint) is a masterpiece.

'This is the best I've done,' Boykie says proudly, 'at least I think so. I think people in South Africa are ready to taste and enjoy something other than Castle. They just need to be given the chance.' Boykie looks like a thin hobbit, and insists I try some of his creation, on the road or not.

I sip half a pint; it's terrific. I debate staying and drowning in lissome blonde female Afrikaner students and Boykie's beer, but sense, or idiocy, prevails. Time to take the road for elsewhere.

I'm heading for the Overberg, the rugged lump of Table Mountain's lower eastern slopes which plugs the gap through which you have to leave Cape Town if you're heading eastwards.

Climbing, winding up into the searing heat of the mountains, moving always towards the Indian Ocean. I've stuffed my map into a front pocket of my jacket, which isn't shut properly, and as the huge buffeting of the Eastern Cape winds combines with my 156 mph speed, the map lifts out and away, fluttering and ripping for an instant before whipping away behind me.

I don't stop.

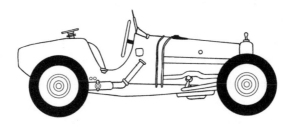

DRUG OF THE NATION

T he wind surprises me, buffeting the big bike around as the Overberg looms, and I climb past weirdly hot versions of Scottish Highland scenery, with names like Glen Fruin tempting me off on narrow detours. If it wasn't for the monkeys which gaze down like gargoyles from the bridges, and the battering heat, I might be heading for Fort William.

There's no time for messing about; the schedule is tight, and so I keep the bike hammering along at 80 to 90 mph, gradually getting used to the belching trucks and meandering *bakkies*, the loaded pedestrians and wandering weans. The road quickly changes from dual carriageway to a bumpy, fast, threatening A-route, and I begin to descend as nightmarish clouds and smoke, from what appear to be faraway belchings from the conflagrations of hell, turn the sky into a dodgily digitised horror movie, a dirty bruised yellow.

I leave the N2 and strike out seawards to Hermanus, one of the top whalewatching centres in Africa, which seems a pleasantly rundown mixture of the bohemian and the geriatric, and thence to Stanford, which I never see, as I turn off before its water-tower-dominated huddle envelops me. I head instead for the avenue of baby trees which leads to the state-of-the-art Birkenhead Brewery, named for a British sailing troopship which sank nearby. They're clearly not big on omens, the management.

The gorgeous Charmaine shows me round. I can see she is unimpressed by the sweat-stained and stinking T-shirt unveiled when I remove my exterior layers. But hospitality flows, in the form of the brewery's own excellent spring water. And a little beer, just for the taste, obviously. I explain that I'm over from the UK to do this assignment for *GQ*.

'Is it all magazine journalism you do in the Yeeew Keeeay?'

I'm desperate to impress, so I casually drop in the magic word 'television'. I've been presenting a car show, I mention. You know, test drives, Aston Martins, Lamborghinis, that sort of thing. Charmaine looks half impressed. As if she sort of believes me. Maybe.

It's the truth, though. A regional television car show, one of several you can pick up on satellite, if you tune into the testosterone-soaked *Men and Motors* section and avoid the silicone breasts, or check out *Discovery Home and Leisure* at certain times of the day. They're made everywhere . . . Ireland, Yorkshire, Scotland, Wales. Car shows, all of them featuring male presenters haunted by the wandering, uneasy spirit of Jeremy Clarkson, all unwilling to believe they're actually being paid (sometimes very little) to drive fast, expensive motors and burble about them on the box. It's mid-life-crisis, menopausal television, and sometimes you can see the desperation in the eyes of the test drivers, as their hair and hopes fall away, and they pray that God will kill Tiff Needel or the baldy one who's just had a hair transplant, the naff so-and-so, so that maybe, just maybe, they'll get to be on *Top Gear* and possibly therefore have sex with that insufferable girl with the hyphen. In a Lamborghini.

If they watch carefully, though, they'll notice that former *Top Gear* regulars, grown old, grey and doddery, are put out to pasture on these regional or satellite shows, filmed on domestic digicams by researchers, bad lighting ruthlessly revealing their sagging jowls. Those who live by telly will eventually embarrass themselves by it. Unless they get plastic surgery.

The show I presented, and am still kind of involved with, is called *Wheelnuts*. My current occasional role is as bike tester, as very few people who have motorcycle licences are practised in the art of talking and riding at the same time. This is something I have been doing for years, as since childhood I have talked to myself. Especially on the road.

In cars, people tend not to hear you when you shout and swear and commentate on your own and others' actions: *Right, you great arse, don't jerk the wheel, that's it, smoothly, good grief, look at that Porsche, what a dickhead . . . hey, dickhead! Only tossers drive Porsches! Okay, now, third gear, that's it . . . just pull out, better signal, all right . . . Bloody hell, should've looked in the mirror, you idiot . . .*

Which is all very well if your car is reasonably well insulated from the outside world. But with the 2CV I once owned, complete with its full-length roller blind of a sunroof, I would sometimes find myself in a Glasgow traffic jam, bellowing out something like: *Awwwl right now, baby, it's a . . . look at the bum on that stupid cyclist, for goodness' sake, some people should be banned from wearing lycra. Hey! Shiny Arse! Bum bum bum bum bum . . .*

Only to find that the object of such attention had been listening. And if a cyclist chooses to hit a 2CV with something more solid than the car itself – say, his hand – much damage may ensue. Citroën 2CVs have been written off after colliding with a seagull. While parking.

On a motorbike, especially wearing a full-face helmet, talking to yourself thankfully produces nothing more than a dull, muffled jabbering, and so people don't tend to look askance at you. They do, however, if you try and answer a mobile phone while still wearing a crash helmet.

Anyway, *Wheelnuts*. I fell into it, really, I'm a hack, a wordsmith for hire who churns out columns for newspapers, radio programmes for those in the BBC I haven't offended during my time as a radio critic (smart move,

Tom). I've done bits and pieces of telly over the years, but it's never been my main source of either income or satisfaction. It's fun, though. Or rather, it's fun when it's not excruciatingly boring. TV crews comprise some of the most genial, sociable people on earth – they have to be in order to get along with egomaniac presenters, producers and directors – and travelling, eating and working with them is usually a source of good conversation, gossip and extreme drunkenness. Unfortunately for the presenter, actually filming or videoing or digitally capturing what may end up as a seven-minute sequence can involve two days of standing around. Or, if you're lucky, sitting around. And as you age, hangovers represent not only a serious threat to your driving capabilities, but leave your face looking like the surface of the moon. Or worse, like Jeremy Clarkson's.

Sure, in a car programme, you can find yourself sitting around in a very, very desirable piece of motorised hardware, but in the end an Aston Martin driven up and down an airstrip thirty or forty times at the behest of a director on the other end of a walkie-talkie becomes nothing more than a posh armchair in a very cramped room, linked to a very poor computer game with boring visuals. Expensively.

So. Motoring telly just sort of happened to me: I received a telephone call from a producer at Scottish Television, who happened to have attended the same school in the same small Ayrshire town I had. Marr College, I salute you! My dad had been her dentist. And so Heather remembered *Spirit of Adventure*, that I had ridden a motorbike and sidecar without appearing to fall off, and talked as well. Next minute, I was off on a motoring freebie to St Tropez.

I thought I'd died and gone to heaven. Well, I thought I was going to die, actually, when the British Airways jet lurched up from Heathrow bound for Nice. Because I was flying club class, and, really, I felt God was certain to take revenge on me for enjoying myself too much. I mean, champagne for breakfast?

Actually, this was nothing. My co-presenter at the time, Kaye Adams, had told me of a previous trip to Mallorca with the cream – or should I say, yoghurt, or possibly dodgy goat's cheese – of the Scottish motoring press. She was the only woman, a matter which exercised the latent lasciviousness and misogyny of the middle-aged male journalists in attendance. What the hell could a woman know about cars? By the time the group arrived on the island of Michael Douglas and Catherine Zeta Jones, vast quantities of alcohol had been consumed by everyone except Kaye and the film crew, exacerbating the suspicion with which the scribblers regarded the 'spies' from STV. One wobbling journo, absolutely steamboats, refused to accept the car he was offered by the endlessly co-operative PR people. 'S'no the right fuckin' colour,' he slurred. 'Cannae 'spect me tae drive that shite. Ah want a red yin.' And then, turning to the astonished Kaye, he winked and said, 'Treat the bastards as if you've got some fuckin' integrity. That's the ticket!'

The truth is, motoring journalism is the last outpost of freebiedom, the biggest scam in newspapers. Car companies have colossal sums to spend on press and promotion, and compete to hold model launches in the best hotels in the world. Bar none. I mean, I ended up in Le Byblos in St Tropez for the sake of a Lexus something or other; George Michael had just vacated my room. Becoming a motoring journalist on one of the nationals, or managing to swing it on a weekly or regional paper so that you do car testing on top of your normal courts and councils, is like winning the lottery. Suddenly, you are being invited to fly club class to all sorts of glorious destinations across the globe, stay in top hotels, eat and drink and be entertained copiously at someone else's expense. Or you might be lent a car – or indeed a motorbike – for long periods of time, during which you can pretend to all and sundry that you're rich enough to actually afford, say, a . . . well. Actually I'd better not say.

Understandably, these are perks not only much sought-after, but carefully protected by the cartel of motoring writers in receipt of them. There are 'guilds' of motoring writers, and belonging to one will allow you almost complete access to the goodies of the automotive world, whether you work for *The Times* or the *Stornoway Gazette*. Entrance to such a society can be even more difficult than joining the Freemasons. Sometimes, it's virtually the same thing.

Of course, the really dodgy practices of the past have been stamped upon by the new breed of newspaper management. The Midlands evening paper motoring correspondent who annually received on loan a brand new motor from the local factory, and was expected to write incisive, investigative news stories about the likes of industrial relations at the plant, was eventually asked if he considered such a freebie in any way compromising to his editorial integrity. He didn't understand the question.

But strange extravagances are still on offer, and accepted, widely. There is the well-known motoring writer who insists that his wife accompanies him on all the groovy trips – though not always, I may add in fairness, at the expense of the car companies involved, or not entirely. I was at one of the two-day launch extravaganzas mounted by Honda for their S2000 sports convertible – each launch lasts for weeks, with shifts of hacks from all over the place arriving and departing, arriving and departing, drinking and getting drunk and being arrested again on the Riviera. We were slightly late in leaving, and thus witnessed what the PR folk clearly hoped we would not: the arrival, for the weekend, in a private plane, of a hand-picked selection of British motoring hacks and their wives or partners. Among them were not one, but two *Top Gear* presenters and their loved ones. Some questioning revealed that this was not a road test, and no one was expected to write or broadcast anything about the trip. The lucky, lucky VIP hacks were just given a car, some goodies (pens, hats, souvenirs), fed, watered and entertained for a weekend, no strings attached.

'It's just a kind of a thankyou,' one of the Honda people told me, as we were hustled aboard a rattly transport plane with some seats hurriedly bolted in, and decanted to Nice and home.

And the strange thing is that the Honda S2000 is not a good car. It is a truly magnificent one, packed with technological brilliance, style and sheer, unadulterated good-time brio. I'm quite happy to say so, even if Honda never choose to say 'thank you' to me. Though a key-ring would be nice.

Anyway, back to my own first motoring freebie. St Tropez (big favourite,

St Tropez), in a Lexus IS200. We all arrived at Nice Airport, where we were given alcohol, food and one of those multimedia slide-show lecture things no one outside of corporate marketing thinks are any good whatsoever. There was a truly repulsive photographer there, one of the school of hacks who think that vast beer bellies go nicely with tight stonewash jeans and artificially distressed leather jackets. Suntanned a deep orangey-purple, he was viciously rude about Lexus and the Japanese, and to one of the nicest people there, a fairly elderly journo with a regional daily broadsheet who was considerate and helpful to me in a way which took me right back to my early days in journalism, when that sort of thing happened.

Maybe it's being Scottish, some deep-seated remnant of childhood Calvinism, or years at the wordface of thankless hard news reporting, but there's something about this conspicuous, utterly shameless and often successful buying up of hacks with luxury and booze that makes me want to pour petrol over the lovely Lexuses or Fords or Hondas they offer you and strike a match. Instead, what I did, being petty and devious, was on principle to thrash the Lexus I was given to within an inch of its existence, and then deprogram the satellite navigation systems so the next journalist would get hopelessly lost. Or even more hopelessly lost than I had with the system in full working order.

Anyway, that's television. What else can I tell you about my brief experience of on-screen motoring? The time a fleet of hot hatches had the paint stripped off their wheel arches by over-enthusiastic cornering on a gravel drive? Well, it wasn't me. Becoming so tired and fed up while filming a Ducati 996 that I let the bloody thing fall over while stationary at traffic lights, and was unable to get it up again unaided? Imitating a dog for a piece about pet seatbelts? The ex-British Army colonel who spends his retirement in the Highlands building exotically and fiendishly expensive pedal cars, and who scared me senseless by taking me for a spin in his home-made 3.5-litre roadster, made out of bits of old taxi cabs? And who owns a vintage fire engine, whose bell he likes to ring at frequent intervals? Bertie o' Brindister, tractor collector? The Simmer Dim motorcycle rally, at which people became more drunk than would have been believed possible. Meeting Davy Jones, the owner of DMA Software, the man who gave the world Grand Theft Auto? Davy had a barn full of several Porsches, a purple Lamborghini Diablo, four or five motorcycles, a tuned Nissan Skyline (700 bhp) and much more. Presumably he still has. What's worse, he seemed perfectly happy and nice with it. He even does his bit for Dundee's music scene, employing local pub musicians to provide the soundtracks for his games. He has a room in his house equipped with twelve linked, state-of-the-art computers so he and his pals can race together. Of course I had a shot.

See what I mean? Sometimes working in TV can be a right sickener.

Talking of sickness, we were once filming in Rome where, for reasons not relevant to this tale, I was unable to drink alcohol. Instead I drank foul mineral water smelling of rotten eggs, which provoked diarrhoea and vomiting of the most spectacular and debilitating kind. During the day's filming, I was forced to call several halts for the sake of emergency bowel and gut evacuation, and my light-coloured trousers meant that, in the end (this is disgusting, but I am honouring the relationship of trust which exists between us, assuming you've stuck it out thus far and aren't just browsing in a bookshop, you sneaky cheapskate) careful camera positioning was necessary in order to avoid embarrassing brownish revelations.

It was crap anyway, that Volvo S70 cabriolet thingy, so if the cream leather of the seats was somewhat spotted, tough shit.

Anyway, we ended up high in the hills above Rome, eating in a pizzeria where they didn't sell pizza, and gave us ciabatta covered in blue mould. I was, inevitably, sick. Back at the Palazzo where we were staying (nothing less will do for motoring media mouthpieces), we took double portions of every freebie we could get hold of (Ray Ban sunglasses, amazing pens in alloy cases, hats, steering wheels, that sort of thing) and left. I managed to get hold of some Immodium at the airport.

Jeremy Clarkson was there, by the way. And if you think he's a really peculiar shape, wears awful clothes and is going bald . . . you're right. The bastard turned out to be quite funny and reasonably friendly too, though. Which was a major disappointment.

Towards the end of filming the second series of *Wheelnuts*, I became seriously fed up with the whole thing. The hanging around, the being away from home. (Produced in Glasgow, the show also involved, as we have seen, considerable gadding about. Living as I do in the Shetland Islands, this made family life a tad awkward.) I lived, during filming, in a friend's house in Glasgow, ate Chinese takeaways and saw lots of movies. For basic transport, I had the Volvo 340, bought for £500, though I ended up spending a further £350 just to make it safe. The family came down for a break in Argyll, and we met on the shores of Loch Awe, where we were bitten by midges, miserably, for two weeks. My wife was then running a Volvo 740 estate, which nearly went on fire through spilling power-steering fluid onto the exhaust.

I couldn't go home with the wife and weans, because I had agreed, for a telly travel show, to ride a Triumph Tiger around the Highlands in a heatwave. I hated what should have been an absolutely brilliant three days. Sailing into Tobermory as the sunlight faded on a beautiful day just made me even more angry with life, the universe and everything. It was time for a change. I told the producers I would not be available for a third series, and headed home. Of course, later I changed my mind.

So here I am, hacking for a glossy magazine, getting incredibly painful inner thighs from the gigantic BMW's saddle, and generally wishing I was somewhere else entirely. If you think I spend far too much time in that self-pitying vein, well, it passes. As you will see. Stick with me.

Birkenhead's rather flash building houses not just a brewery and bottling plant but also a restaurant and pub, and bus tours are already making it a regular port of call. The food – I gorge myself on octopus, chips, salad and a variety of spicy sauces – is excellent, and the single main beer (there is an Oktober Ale I'd love to try) is very good. I feel better. Self-pity? Moi? Piss off!

Odd, business, though, the Birkenhead bubbles.

'We go for the champagne bubbles,' says Charmaine, which means that, when really cold, Birkenhead can seem flat. It also means you can quaff a lot. I don't. Though I think Charmaine is warming to me. Must be the pheromones in my sweat-stained T-shirt. Then I remember that I hand-washed the shirt in question the previous night in the Cape Town hotel room. Perhaps Charmaine goes for the aroma of Ariel Rapide, oil, perspiration and unsuccessful rinsing.

Inevitably, there's a Scot in the bar. Jimmy. His wife is Valerie, and they are in their early fifties, sun-damaged from too many years here in the land of the off-white. He loves bikes, but his sons aren't interested. He owns an old Triumph T140 he wants to put a Yamaha engine into, which sounds like blasphemy to me.

'Biking's really big in Johannesburg,' he says.

Will I be safe there, I wonder aloud.

'No,' he replies.

'Oh, I don't know,' says Charmaine. 'I lived in Johannesburg all my life, and never got into any trouble at all. Then I came down here last year, and my car's been broken into three times in Hermanus.'

There is that usual white South African humphing and harrumphing, and I can sense a *bangpraat* moment. *Bangpraat* is the exchange by socialising whites of their experience, of violence in the new South Africa, and how they've just been raped/beaten up/robbed/know someone who has. So I change the subject. Where have Jim and his wife driven from?

'We've just come down the R325,' he says. 'The fire's right down at the road, but you should be all right.'

Fire? What fire?

'Oh, we get a lot of forest fires,' smiles Charmaine. 'I don't know if a motorbike is the best thing, really.'

It is, however, my only thing.

Jim leans on the bar and tells me about going home to Fife, where his brothers are into bikes, still. 'But they won't come here,' he says, wistfully.

'Best biking country in the world, and they won't come over. I keep telling them, but no. Too dangerous. Too much trouble. I don't know.'

I do, though. I know exactly how they feel. Maybe I could sell one of them my bulletproof vest.

Charmaine and I part with a chaste handshake. Perhaps I will be consumed by the fire, I joke. She laughs. *Charmaine, Charmaine, and I thought you cared for me.* I fill up my water bottle, strap everything onto the bike (in my entire trip through South Africa, I will leave the bike unattended many times, with all my luggage bungeed onto it, and nothing will ever be taken; nor will I be mugged, raped, accosted or even spoken to in a loud voice) and head for the flames of hell. Hell, what else is a man to do? As Woody Allen once memorably said in his long-forgotten movie *What's Up, Tiger Lily?*, 'Death is my bread and danger my butter . . . no, no, danger is my bread and death is my butter . . . death and danger are my various breads and various butters.'

Might as well start buttering.

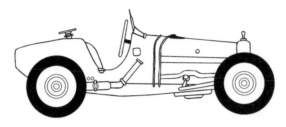

FIRE DOWN BELOW (AND GENERAL STICKINESS)

The smell hits you first, then the smoking darkness on both sides of the road. It's like being in a film. The road is a river of grey with blackness on both sides. Not long ago, maybe a day, I don't know, this would have been impassable without risking serious burns, not to mention possibly an exploding petrol tank. Should I turn back to Charmaine's smile and very, very short skirt? But she's already forgotten me. Of course she has. I push on. Miles to go before I sleep, and all that.

A giant tortoise crosses the road, still alive. Not, as far as I can see, blackened. I avoid hitting it, and, as I climb up into scrubby, rocky hills, the blackness along the verges vanishes. But there's still a hazy shimmer in the air, still the aroma of destruction. Then I spot what looks like orange undergrowth over to the left. A thin line of reddish-yellow bushes, their leaves bright against the grey-green rock and stunted trees. Closer, and it's Moses and the burning bushes. Fortunately, the wind is blowing away from me, and I can watch the fire's slow but certain advance from a position of safety. The line of flames moves in a slow, almost stately fashion, regular, precise, hypnotic. There is no sign of firefighters or, indeed, anyone else at all. Occasionally there's the sinewy flicker of a monkey close to me, but no one and nothing seems overly concerned. It's hypnotic: I could stay and watch this all day, but I move on before the wind changes.

One of the central myths of car sex involves the vaginal spasm which leads to two adulterers being joined together in something altogether less holy than matrimony. The fire brigade is called, the car (brand new, owned by cuckolded husband) is cut up and the couple eventually freed, so that the wonders of medical science can have a go at separating them. Presumably without recourse to angle grinders and scalpels.

So we have evil carnal conjoining carried out within the confines of that sexual object the car, and leading not only to the emasculation of the illicit male lover through spasmodic vulvic seizure, but to the emasculation of the betrayed husband, metaphorically, through the acetylene torch attentions of the firemen. And women.

Great story. Like all fairytales it carries a hefty sexual and moral meaning, but it's not, in the factual sense, true. It didn't really happen.

On the other hand, I did once buy a car purely and simply in order to have sex in it. This vehicle – of all things, an MG Maestro – was aimed at two women in particular, one in the short term, one in the long. Both liked the idea of being seen in respectable cars, but one was interested in short-term shagology, while the other wanted a decent middle-class long-term relationship. Actually, I later bought a house just to impress that woman, which did, sort of. Unfortunately, by that time I was more impressed with someone else entirely.

Those were the days of rampant promiscuity, and the interesting thing is that while I failed to have sex with either of the vehicularly targeted women in the MG itself, the car undoubtedly aided my campaign to gain entry to their beds. Before long I was deservedly duped and dumped by one of them, while I quite shamefully and cynically betrayed and dumped the other.

I was, not to put too fine a point on it, a real bastard in those days, the early '80s, when Glasgow's club scene had yet to encounter HIV and the nights offered rock music, alcohol, the occasional mild herbal or chemical high and the prospect of sex. Cars were for the most part a handicap to sexual success, as at three in the morning post-club couplings depended on alcohol and alcohol required a taxi cab for transportation deep into the bohemian heart of the West End. And very few of the women I met in those frenzied *Melody Maker* years, guest-listing from gig to party to club to bedroom, were interested in cars as anything more than representations of male status. Like doormen, they eyed shoes and cars and made decisions about permitting entry on the basis of style and cost. Much in the same way as I eyed them.

Passing my driving test was, and had always been seen by me as, a passport to women. Fondling, kissing and having sex (in the innocent sense of the word) in the passenger seat. At seventeen, not only did I not really know what sex involved, I thought sexual politics might be something to do with dirty jokes down the Labour Club. I didn't think about politics at all. Instead, I thought about religion. And rock music.

So my first girlfriend was fifteen, lived in far-off Galloway, and had been met ('got off with' was the prevalent phrase) at a Christian evangelistic mission in her home village. It was a pure, innocent, long-distance love, and I saw her infrequently. Once when she travelled to Ayr on the bus. And once when I made the epic seventy-mile journey to see her in Castle Douglas. On my Honda 50. We spent two hours walking hand in hand and occasionally practising dribble-free kissing, then I rode the tiny buzz-box home. One gallon of petrol for 150 miles and a snog. Not a bad bargain, though my bum was sore for a week, and not for any sexual reason. That Honda saddle was hard as hell.

With Edith, while there may have been trouser-straining engorgements, there was no guilt, no fumbling or emitting. It was a squelch-free relationship. No hydraulics. But we did kiss in a car. Twice. Once when I picked her up from a rendezvous with her parents halfway down the A75 for a Rolling Stones gig at the Apollo in Glasgow (1973, *Goats Head Soup* tour, Mick Jagger in a wig, Billy Preston on keyboards) and once with all her pals when I took her out to a Ten Years After gig and then deposited her (and the friends she'd come to Glasgow with) back somewhere on the south side. Tongues came into play. Fortunately we'd both had pickled onions with our chips. The intention to kiss was signalled, in those days before inertia reel seatbelts, by the casual metallic snick of a released buckle. Followed by the lean-in across the gearstick.

INTERNAL COMBUSTION

Edith and I, though, were going our separate ways. It took another visit to Prestwick Airport (in my MG 1100) on one of those manic Hogmanay whirls through Ayrshire after the bells, sober and in a paroxysm of sexual-cum-religious mania, though hardly even knowing it, to establish my next step up the ladder of love. She was beautiful, she was older, she worked in insurance. We made frenzied clothes-on love on her mum's sofa, orgasm was achieved and I thought pregnancy, not to mention being eternally cursed by God and my mum, was in the offing.

While waiting for this to happen, we went on two-couple necking runs with friends, one in the back seat, one in the front. Couples, that is. Religion meant that things never got, so to speak, out of hand. Frankly, nothing came to hand, without the muffling provided by several layers of cloth. But such was the excitement generated that I spent most of that year in a state of genital solidity. It made it possible to hold the steering wheel without using your hands.

It looked serious. Her dad lent me his Cortina GT. My dad bought me a Fiat 500. But she had no love for the Rolling Stones. I met a girl with an Austin 1100 and got engaged to be married. Two and a half years later, we did. I talked of buying a motorbike. She said she would divorce me. As we weren't married at the time, I took this threat seriously. For a long time, I didn't think about bikes at all.

I remember us standing outside our house seven years later in front of the Citroën 2CV we had jointly bought, brand new, for £2,000. Not for the first time, it wouldn't start, and we were screaming at each other. Usually, we removed the two (count 'em) spark plugs and warmed them in the oven. This had been tried, but hadn't helped. Pushing, jump starts . . . in the end, choked with rage at the 2CV, I just walked away. I came back that night from work, but the walking away never stopped from then on.

Be warned: Citroën 2CVs are very bad for relationships. For one thing, they are unreliable and terrible at firing up in damp weather (for which, read: a rain shower within the last year). This leads to disharmony. Also, they are French. They were designed to include the vengeful spirit of a betrayed female resistance hero who sacrificed her life in fighting the

Nazis because her lover ran off with another woman. They militate against happiness. They act to create discord and argument. The full-length sunshine roof blows off, while you shout at your partner, like the eyelid of God suddenly opening. They are allegories of bad love: under-powered, badly made, flimsy (I once slammed the bootlid of ours on a suitcase, leaving a perfect imprint of the case in the metal), attractive in a superficial, short-term way. They do not last. They decay quickly. They break down. In the wrong circumstances, they can kill you. If anything hits them, they disintegrate as if they were made of wet cardboard. Curiously, my last and present wife also split up with her long-term lover in a 2CV. I rest my case. She kept the thing, but traded it in for a VW Golf before I met her.

More than the Citroën and my marriage fell apart. Life in general did. My career as a religious singer and evangelist vanished like spark plugs down the inaccessible cowling of a 600cc 2CV motor. I worked in a hi-fi shop. Rode a bicycle. Motorbikes had been long forgotten. I drove a horrid Honda Civic, supplied by the shop, and a worse Renault 11 which was repaired by a friendly body shop using strips of plastic. I found this out when, having been ransomed, if not saved, by rock'n'roll and the discovery that you could make money and get girls by writing about bands, not to mention get into gigs free, I drove a much-obsessed-over rock chick out into the country one New Year's morning and totalled the Renault 11 into a brand new Renault Fuego. Near Strathblane. I had consumed over a bottle of vodka in the previous twelve hours. No one was hurt. The Fuego looked better with a large dent in its front wing, though the owner did not think so. The 11 looked as if it had been caught in a volcanic eruption of rust. The rock chick was not impressed. When we split up, I threatened to drive my limping Renault into a wall and take myself out. She slammed the door so hard it fell off.

I knew one woman whose passion was to make love in the back seat (not the front, the back) of a Hillman Avenger I briefly owned. She was also fond of Polaroid photographs and videos taken during sex, as well as the odd bit of bondage. I'm not saying that these accoutrements of the carnal act didn't interest or excite me. It's just that her attachment to the slippery vinyl of the Avenger made me wonder if there was any future in the relationship. After all, a woman who became seriously excited by a mouldering old car assembled in Linwood was bound to have some question marks over her character. The nearly dead Vauxhall Viva I briefly owned (sold for £25 to a man who insisted I prove it could go by driving it a mile to Partick Cross – it took two litres of brake fluid to achieve that) had the opposite effect on another girlfriend, who refused point blank to be seen dead with me in it. And even kissing was out of the question inside its murky interior. 'It smells of dead pigeons,' she said. Though how she knew that, I have no idea.

Eventually I made the belated discovery every male makes in the end. The worrying one. That women like their men to be in some way similar to their fathers. The ones who want you to wear Old Spice aftershave because it reminds them of their dad are not as disturbingly strange as they may appear. But the ones who want to have sex in a Hillman Avenger because their dad had one may well be. On the other hand they may not. Anyway, it didn't last. Neither did the relationship.

Let's just say that time passed. I met the girl, or woman, who used to have motorbikes and everything changed. Everything.

The BMW swoops along the coastline towards Knysna, passing glorious beach after glorious beach, until in the immediate run into the town, the geography begins to remind me weirdly of Argyll, at the top of the Kintyre peninsula. Only with elephants. Well, there are supposed to be elephants. No one's seen any for years. There are signs saying 'beware', though. So I beware.

Maybe it's the rain. It plummets down, but my expensive Cordura top keeps most of the dampness out. I hate motorcycle boots, for obscure aesthetic reasons: they make me feel like some Oswald Mosley replicant. Instead, I wear steel-toed Caterpillar Doc Marten imitations, with a gap between their tops and the bottom of my leather trousers which has left my ankles sodden. I am reminded of a pal back in Shetland, a member of the excellent Zetland Motorcycle Club (you have to be thirty-five plus to join), who memorably praised the waterproof qualities of his new motorcycle boots with the words: 'When I piss in them, it stays put, and I can keep my feet warm.'

Knysna is lovely. I'm staying on the waterfront, a kind of cutdown version of the mammoth Cape Town harbour development, and the new Protea – a member of the massive South African Hotel chain – is a vision in blond oak and stainless steel. Secure parking for the BMW. I prowl the piers and eat excellent Cape salmon at a place called the Dry Dock, but the old town's more interesting, especially after a night's sleep. On a Saturday morning with the warm rain pouring down and crowds of people idly shopping.

Knysna has always had a reputation as a laid-back artists' community, and there are still signs of that amongst the upmarket mini-mall and trendy bars and boutiques. On this Saturday, the place has an integrated feel, unlike anywhere else I've been in South Africa. Black and white mix freely and the seething bus station feels . . . like Africa. The gentrification stops here. It's just that, as ever, it's the whites who look rich and the blacks who look poor.

This is where Mitchell's, the brewer's pub back in Cape Town, started, but there's nothing gentrified about their HQ, in an industrial unit next to a timber yard. A hand-lettered notice on the timber business says in English and Xhosa: no work available. Mitchell's is hard to find, but worth the search. Security on my mind, I park the bike within sight of the bush-shrouded doorway, and leave it to soak. Under dour, grey Scottish skies, it's now pissing down.

As the rain rattles on the tin roof, I perch on a stool at the tiny bar which has been built for tasting purposes, and work through what in Scotland they would call a pony (a quarter of a pint, and once an illegal measure) of Forrester's, Bosun's Bitter – both of which I tried back in Cape Town – and the stunning Raven Stout, which is more like a Scottish stout than Murphy's or Guinness. Mitchell's Old 90 shilling ale is great too, malty and dark, like a Belhaven from home.

Mitchell's tends not to travel that far from home – East London's Tug and Ferry is about the limit – because it's unpasteurised, but Knysna locals are able to come in and get their plastic bottles refilled. A dozen or so do just that as I wait. Big *braai* plans for the night, I presume, if the rains stop.

Four Australian surfer types are getting slowly and pleasantly pissed, while the raven-haired goddess in charge of the pub, all denim cut-offs and a distinctly damp T-shirt (why are brewery women all gorgeous here?) is kindness itself, charging me nothing at all for the beer I consume in such tiny quantities.

I could stay all day, but Port Alfred awaits. It's a long wet slog, initially, through spectacularly mountainous country, the Tsitsikammaberge, past gorge after gorge, bungee jump after bungee jump, one of them claiming to be the deepest in the world. Could well be. Forest follows wood, and petrol is running dangerously low when I finally come across a service area near Kareedouw. I still can't get used to the bigness of South Africa and the comparative sparseness of things like garages. There is a well-equipped huddle of carry-out, souvenir shop and petrol station, and the hamburgers are great. During the whole journey I will eat dubious food from all kinds of places, and never get ill. But, hey, I'm no intrepid investigative explorer. Maybe I didn't try hard enough.

In the car park, I spot a Morris Minor convertible, immaculate in that bluey-grey colour I remember so well from my Uncle John's rotting example. But this has been restored and, inside, red leather glints. The owner is nowhere in sight. I wonder about the kind of South African who restores, at doubtless massive expense, such a personification of British-ness. It's nostalgia for home taken to automotive extremes.

Yet the car represents much more. To restore a Morris Minor you order parts from Sri Lanka, where a low-tech production line has been set up, dozens of natives hand-beating panels for the worldwide retro market. India still makes the old Morris Oxford my dad had, called a Hindustani Ambassador, and they are being exported to Britain. A taxi-driver in Lerwick once excitedly showed me the Hindustani brochure, and claimed he was about to order one.

All over the world, little pockets of old technology are trapped, still churning out their pieces of practicality for home markets, items which have kitsch value elsewhere. There are the Enfield Bullet motorcycles, also in India. The Ural, Dneipr and Jupiter motorbikes of the Ukraine and Russia, based on the BMW designs appropriated when the Soviets overran German factories at the end of The Second World War. Unassembled Morris Marinas turn up occasionally from warehouses abroad and are snapped up by idiot collectors in the UK. It's a weird industry, motor manufacture, more and more concentrated in the hands of multinationals, but with that desperate search for history, for identity and individuality on the part of ordinary consumers leading to the existence of these odd automotive backwaters. Most of these cultish cars and bikes are crap. I once test drove a restored Minor and nearly killed myself with its useless drum brakes.

Car manufacture, of course, all began in Scotland. Didn't you know that? You probably realised that various crucial parts of the whole motoring experience owe their existence to Scots. The first pedal bicycle, without which there would, clearly, be no motorcycle or even moped: Kirkpatrick MacMillan of Dumfries, 1839. The first pneumatic tyre? You're thinking the thoroughly Caledonian John Boyd Dunlop; but, no, the first patent was lodged by Robert William Thompson of Stonehaven in 1846. Dunlop re-invented the inflatable tyre in 1888 and founded the firm which still bears his name. But what would have been the point of pneumatic tyres without a decent road on which to seek punctures? Step right up, John Loudon MacAdam. Tarmacadam, ta very much.

Ah, but the car? Everybody knows the modern automobile was invented in 1885 by a German, Karl Benz. Sort of. Maybe. But lots of people in many countries had been messing about with horselessness for years, and one of the very first was Scottish engineer William Murdoch.

In 1784 Murdoch was in Cornwall working for Bolton and Watt, a company specialising in pumping engines, powered of course by steam. He built a tiny three-wheeled vehicle powered by an alcohol-burning steam engine. It worked well, as long as it ran on a level surface, and was demonstrated widely. One evening, the Vicar of Redruth saw it, clanking and belching out smoke, steam and sparks, and understood immediately that he had met with the Devil himself. Why does my mind turn to the Citroën 2CV?

Murdoch decided to head for London and patent this, the first car, but his boss, Matthew Bolton, stopped him, arguing that this valued employee would be wasting his time on his planned next step, which was to build a full-size, passenger-carrying machine. Murdoch went back to stationary engines, but amazingly his little three-wheeler, crude in the extreme, survives today, in Birmingham.

Of course, steam was never going to be the motive force for lightweight road transport, despite hanging on into the 1840s with commercial traction engines in Britain. And, indeed, the internal combustion engine which gives its name to this book arrived in the 19th century, courtesy of a Belgian, Etienne Lenoir. His crude two-stroke coal gas engine was as naught, though, compared to the four-stroke produced by Frenchman Alphonse Beau De Rochas in 1862. Not that it worked properly. It was, after all, French. The first properly functioning four-stroke petrol engine was demonstrated in 1878 by the German Nikolaus Otto, and the application of the internal combustion engine to transportation was also brought to us by the Germans.

At the same time, another German, Gottlieb Daimler, son of a baker, was experimenting with a petrol-engined car, using a two-cylinder engine as opposed to Benz's single-lung affair. His first vehicle ran in 1889.

The rest, as they say, is history. The world's history. My history. Port Elizabeth is where South Africa's motor industry is centred. As you pass it on the N2, down by the Indian Ocean shore, where hundreds of people with gigantic fishing rods line the sea walls, it sits, suppurating and stinking in the blustery sun, the very image of the damage the automobile can do.

It's the worst industrial smell I have encountered since those childhood days passing through Colville's works at Cambuslang or the noxious pit bings of South Ayrshire. Great tracts of land lie discoloured and abandoned. This is where history can lead, where the brilliant invention of a Scot and two Germans has taken us. I rev the big BMW, let the catalyser attached to the engine take me, relatively cleanly, out and onwards, north; forever north.

Not as far north as I'd like to be, though. In Shetland, where I came in 1986 on the offchance that a girl I'd met in a Glasgow bar might let me live in her large rented house. For a while. I had a horribly rusted Ford Cortina Estate, loaded with all my wordly goods, no job, and just a few freelance contacts in the music press.

In truth, I was already in love with both Susan and Shetland, a place with a landscape so bare and brutal that you either hate it for life or end up knowing you're going to have to live there. Two week-long visits and I was seduced. By the landscape, that is. And its culture. The music, yes, the Viking legends, the amazing, welcoming necessity to blow the winter darkness apart with the light and love of having a good time. And with the attitude towards transport. Shetland loves its motor vehicles, and especially its motorbikes. Until the early 1960s, the motorbike was the staple means of transport for the rural crofter, often purchased with the cash earned from a hard Arctic winter at the whaling. Ariels, Nortons, Greaveses, Velocettes . . . they were loved and cared for, raced and used for everything from wedding transport (with sidecars) to carting sheep to market.

Then came the Morris Minor and the Mini: small cheap cars were suddenly accessible, and the bikes were, almost overnight, abandoned. In barns, sheds or just left lying in the lee of a crofthouse wall. Just before local folk began cottoning onto the fact that they might be valuable, and a thriving vintage bike scene began to develop, several dealers from England and Ireland arrived. The bastards bought up every trashed bike they could find, and headed off on the ferry to restore and sell them. Look for number plates beginning PS, and you'll recognise these acquisitions.

Now, though, bikes are big with a new moneyed generation who use them for thrills, not necessity. The Simmer Dim rally, held each midsummer in the all-night daylight of Shetland's midnight sun, attracts hundreds of local and foreign bikers to a weekend of almost inconceivable indulgence. I belong to the Zetland Motorcycle Club, a relaxed group of somewhat aged and battered bikers, many, like me, in need of losing some weight. We are, of course, all sixteen at heart, hopelessly immature wearers of ill-advised leather jackets.

And then there's the car culture. Some of the more isolated Shetland islands have neither policemen nor MOT stations, which means you can drive almost anything on them. And people do. I have personally been in a car on the island of Unst which was stopped, and I'm not joking, by putting your feet through the floor and grinding your soles down on the tarmac. Admittedly, this only worked at very slow speeds, but as the car – a Volvo 340 – could do no more than 15 mph this wasn't too much of a problem. And, anyway, the driver had usually consumed a rather large quantity of local home-brew before he could actually operate the thing.

Elsewhere, young blades with cash from fishing or oil will thrash their brand-new BMWs around island circuits late at night, high on whatever they can get. And poorer kids will dice with danger and death and the local police in much less glamorous machinery.

I once reported on a court case where the police pursued two young men at speeds of over 120 mph on single-track country roads up and down Shetland for much of a Saturday night, failing to catch them. The sixteen-year-old they eventually accused of leading them this merry dance (yes, sixteen) had just bought the battered Vauxhall Cavalier SRI the cops had been chasing. For £200. In the end, he got off with it. He claimed his pal had been driving, his pal claimed he had. Baffled, the forces of law and order withdrew to lick their wounds and check the engine in their highly tuned Volvo Turbo pursuit car.

The horrific aroma of Port Elizabeth recedes, as does the strange duneland which comes immediately after. I stop for petrol and juice in Colchester, where odd, semi-derelict holiday villages huddle in the shadow of the biggest sand dunes I have ever seen. Then there's a great loop inland before turning back down to the coast, the whole countryside growing increasingly sandy and pale, and Port Alfred. This is surfing territory, and high dunes shelter hidden holiday communities, sleepy refuges from just about everything, including, you get the feeling, law and order.

In Port Alfred I meet Surfin' Vic and his Chinese Jeep. Vic picks me up from the Protea in a vehicle best described as very nearly dead. It has a diesel engine which rattles so much I can feel my fillings coming loose. And Vic has that loping surfer's build, not to mention the goofy smile and languid vowels of an inveterate smoker of good strong dope. *Dagga* grows like crazy around here.

Port Alfred has a kind of good-humoured weirdness about it. Vic's pal Ian is a home-brewer, and we start by sampling some of his efforts. Which are good kit beers made in bins and bottled in his garage. Then it's down to the river bank, where Johan Strydom has only just set up Coelacanth Brewery, here where the first ancient sea-beast was rediscovered in the 1930s.

It's a small but nicely formed brewery, and Johan (I've been warned by Vic that he's a somewhat nippy Afrikaner) is cautiously, then warmly welcoming. There's only one beer – Old Four Legs, as in Coelacanth. I am off the bike, nursing a dreadful cold, so I indulge more than I have so far on this trip. After all, Vic's driving. Sort of. Reeling just slightly, we head off to the house of the legendary Paddy Carolan, ex-fighter pilot and bomb designer. (At one point he shows me a lump of twisted metal and tells me it came from the bombed runway of Baghdad Airport during the Gulf War. 'I helped design this bomb,' he says. 'We may have been the polecats of the world but they still bought our shit!')

Paddy collects beer. He has one of the largest collections of bottled beer in the world, apparently, all housed in a custom designed bar just off his bedroom. He has 2,500 different ales. We drink Castle, which he loves, and eat from trays of nuts provided by Mrs Carolan. Until Vic suddenly notices that the bottom of each tray is alive with ants, much to the embarrassment of our hosts.

'Hey, man! It's protein!' grins Vic, and keeps on eating.

Paddy has toured Europe as an ambassador for Castle, and won't hear a bad word about the stuff. Despite his massive collection of beers – all in unopened bottles – his tastes are simple, ale-wise. There are pictures on the wall of him and his fellow Castle ambassadors (all of whom won a competition to design an unusual receptacle for drinking Castle – Paddy's involved shell casings) crawling on all fours in a strange bellyflop conga line through bars in London, Amsterdam and other parts of Europe. Never have I heard a man be so rude about Namibia's Windhoek beer (they use recycled water), which I think knocks Castle into the proverbial cocked hat.

Paddy and his wife are hospitality personified, despite the ants. We leave amid promises of barbecues, Thai curries and stories of how the Carolans arrived in South Africa originally because Paddy's grandfather 'liked killing Englishmen, and wanted a chance to do it legally' and so went to war on the side of the Boers. Paddy himself went to war in his Mirage jets, dicing with Russians in Angola ('years later, I had a drink with one of the pilots I tried to shoot down'), mock-bombing liners as a favour to the crew, and generally having a high old time. He has cooked for De Klerk and Mandela, he tells me, and will for me the next time, too.

My nose is running like a burn by this time, and Mrs Carolan provides me with a box of man-size tissues. Groggily, I ask Surfin' Vic to take me back to the Protea. On the way back to the hotel, Vic and Ian toke on the biggest, most acrid joint I have seen in years. 'Hey, man, pity you can't get to Port St Johns . . . best dope in the world there . . . make a lot of money, some guys do, running stuff in from there . . .'

I smile, shake hands in that three-grip South African way I still can't get used to.

Surfin' Vic informs me that I should reach Durban easily in six hours from Port Alfred.

'It's over 562 miles,' I mumble.

'Don't stop in Umtata,' he warns, 'I used to live there, and it's not good.'

'Why?' I wonder.

'It just isn't,' he repeats. 'Unpleasant. That bike of yours, you can make it, just crank it up and keep going. And if you hit anything, don't stop.' He pauses. 'Or anyone. There'll be people all over the road, man. Leave at dawn,' he recommends, 'before the day has a chance to heat up.' The advice is dope-fuelled and consequently long-drawn-out, rambling, but well meant.

'Don't stop in the Transkei,' he advises, casually.

I remember the conversations back in Cape Town, about the fact that there hadn't been a hold-up by bandits in the old homelands of the Transkei for, oh, two or three years. Feeling too ill to care much, I crash into bed, drink and aspirin fuelling a dream-haunted sleep.

Dawn is wet and cold, a dreich Highland seaside day. It's like the Moray coast, around Findhorn. Something weird: on the streets are black police and soldiers armed to the teeth. They take no notice of me. I get out of Port Alfred. A strange place. I wonder what's really going on there.

Even at dawn, the R72 to East London is dotted with black figures,

INTERNAL COMBUSTION

crouched by the verge, holding out a single orange, apple or banana for sale, as if it's the last thing on earth they own. Maybe it is.

East London looms, a genuinely attractive town, with a pleasantly shabby, run-down feel. The N2 north of East London is the only South African road the British Foreign Office specifically warns tourists off. At first that seems like daft advice, as a dual carriageway, black with burnt rubber, winds up into the hills. For a mile or two. I race Sunday-morning bikers along it, then abruptly the road narrows, splits, crumbles, and hundreds of people appear on it, walking, loaded with massive head-carried burdens. Going and coming, to and from God knows where. Goats and scrawny sheep wander unhindered, unfenced. Diseased *bakkies*, down on their tyres with ten or more people on board, lumber dangerously along. Just before Tainton I pull out to overtake one and it suddenly swerves to the right. I slam on the brakes, blindly, thoughtlessly reacting, front and back, the way they say you never should on a bike. But the high-tech BMW has ABS, and with that inimitable rattling clatter, it cuts in, bringing the bike to a perfect halt just as the oblivious *bakkie* driver sails off into a side road, skimming my front wheel by millimetres.

After that, despite Vic's advice, I slow down. I have to, because the road becomes almost inconceivably bad. There are gates across it which close off the N2 entirely in case of mud slides, and lines of traffic slip and stumble upwards through endless roadworks, decayed, swept-away tarmac and patches of nothing but dirt. Again, the BMW comes into its own, and I understand why it's South Africa's best-selling motorbike. All I can say is I'm glad I'm not on a lumbering Harley Davidson. No way would that tractorish make of monsterbike have made it through. Despite its size and weight, the BMW is designed for terrain just like this, and I begin to acquire some affection for it. Grudging affection.

Butterworth looms, decayed and battered and throbbing with threat. It was built as an industrial centre for the Transkei; now the factories are falling down, and you have the sense of a society in tatters. How will democracy cope? These are the questions, or some of the questions, that *GQ* South Africa doesn't want answered. It's a magazine which, like much else in the burgeoning ghetto of the RSA economy, contrives to ignore inequality, suffering, death, violence and politics. So I'm allowed to communicate the thrill but not the horrors, the beer but not the reasons for the country's mass alcoholism. And colour? Doesn't exist, man. People are people . . .

The roads are unsurfaced, crowds linger in the litter-strewn streets, and for a white boy on a motorbike it's an exposed place to be. The Transkei, along with other so-called independent homelands (utterly corrupt puppet states run by on-the-take placemen), is where tens of thousands of blacks were forcibly resettled by the apartheid government, and the place is drastically overcrowded still, even under the rule of the new South Africa. The land is eroding at an alarming rate, and the little Zulu thatched huts and their concrete equivalents are so universal that they become the rule rather than a picturesque piece of touristicana.

Butterworth passes, and as Umtata's nearness is signalled by the road turning into a teeming stream of perambulating humanity, I pull into the Shell Ultra City, a seething service area where, for the first time on the trip, I don't feel able to leave the bike unattended. It's midday, and I'm sucking great draughts from my on-board water supply, as young guys drink *sorghum* from plastic two-litre bottles and eye me, I think, in racist paranoia, speculatively. But then, why shouldn't they?

There's no Umtata bypass, so straight through the chaotic centre I go. Truth to tell, it's busy without being particularly worrying, although the traffic is insane. No actual or potential muggers appear to lurk by the robots, or the traffic lights. There is a long stretch of comparatively quiet road which leads me out past Qumbu, where Nelson Mandela has his retirement home. I ponder Alan Titchmarsh and Charlie Dimmock's sojourn here, doing a makeover on Madiba's garden, to what looked to me like a very lukewarm response from the great leader himself. What a sad, tacky, utterly naff idea. Especially amid the poverty and eroded land of the Transkei, where thousands are scratching at patches of bad land for food, not decoration. I doubt that the *Ground Force* team stayed in desperate settlements like Mount Frère – even the *Rough Guide* advises you not to stop there – or worse, Mount Ayliff. For much of the route a couple in a white Volkswagen Golf stay just ahead of me, signalling with their hazard warning lights if any problems are approaching. Animals on the road are the worst – goats without any kind of traffic sense stand, ready to leap straight at you.

Thankfully, I don't run anyone down. When I get back to Scotland, I will read in the *London Review of Books* a long article about a trip made along this same stretch by two South African families with impeccable white liberal intellectual credentials. The first car knocked down a young girl, and they stopped. Immediately, they were surrounded by a crowd carrying *knobkerries* and baying for money. They handed over what they had, and insisted on taking the child, who was conscious and walking, to the hospital in Mount Frère. The hospital, with blocked toilets and wholly inadequate staffing, did less than nothing for the girl. One of the women in the white group sat in her car, nursing a gun. Eventually the two families just made a run for it, bleeding liberal guilt the whole way to Durban.

I'm thinking about my only major collision with a pedestrian, which happened as I was driving a Mini Clubman Estate along Bank Street in the west end of Glasgow, in 1978. My gaze was diverted, just for a millisecond. An old, impossibly fat woman suddenly lurched out from between two parked cars, unheeding of anything on the road. I braked, the screech still echoing in my head, but she hit the bonnet of the little car and flew in slow motion, it seemed, high into the air, turning in a graceful arc before landing against the opposite kerb like a bloated sack of vegetables.

What distracted my attention? What caught my eye in the wing mirror? Would it have made any difference if I had been focusing my entire attention on the road in front of me?

Oh yes. Yes yes yes yes yes . . .

She was conscious and trying to get up when I reached her, my car abandoned in the middle of the narrow road, traffic piling up behind me. Passers-by, in true Glaswegian style, stopped to help her up, as she insisted she was in no pain, she was fine, if someone would just give her a hand to her house, two closes down . . .

Her home help turned up. The old woman was called Agnes Johnson, and she was blind in one eye. Which eye, I wondered, oh God, make it the right one, make it not my fault, make it not my fault. But it was. I knew, just couldn't admit it. Then I noticed her left leg. It had broken at the shin and was at right angles to the rest of her.

I ran to phone for an ambulance and the police, feeling as if the world had ended, other than for my feelings of pain and guilt and fear and sickness. We sat Mrs Johnson down on the kerb, and she chatted cheerfully about how it was all her fault. The police arrived, and the ambulance. She was whisked off, chatting away to the ambulancemen, while a concerned sergeant made me sit down, asked me if I was all right, then told me to drive around the block before coming back to give him my version of events.

'Best to drive immediately after an accident,' he said. 'Otherwise, sometimes you never do.'

Something had caught my eye . . . I didn't tell him that.

'She just walked right out in front of me . . . apparently she's blind in one eye, her home help will tell you . . . I didn't have a chance to react, next thing she was flying through the air . . .'

But something had caught my eye. I told no-one. Didn't mention it to my wife (married at twenty-one, can you believe that?), played a gig in Crieff that evening, drove back to Glasgow to find the whole West End in turmoil, the Grosvenor Hotel in flames. Sent Mrs Johnson flowers at the Western Infirmary, told the insurance assessor I didn't have a chance to avoid her . . . heard she was doing okay. Knowing that whatever happened, the accident would shorten her life. She was eighty.

And what had caused it? Me looking in the wing mirror at a girl in a short skirt. Sex.

At Kokstad the Transkei ends and Natal begins. I recuperate for two hours in a pretty little service station, eating hamburgers and drinking two pints of iced Coke. I have been riding for six-and-a-half hours and am still a long, long way from Durban.

The N2 assumes the character of a rural A-road as it meanders through the hills towards the coast at Port Shepstone. It's quiet, too, a lot of the traffic off on the inland R56 to Pietermaritzburg. But after Port Shepstone, with a heavy hot smell of salt in my nostrils, things start going berserk. After Hibberdene, the N2 turns into a right-enough, gigantic motorway, crammed with cars, trucks, *bakkies* and combi taxis, all driving flat out. I am so tired I can barely hang on as the BMW navigates itself into and out of trouble. I pass two heavy-duty smashes, bloodied bodies on the side of the road. Fruit-sellers line the hard shoulder. Somehow I take the right exit and thankfully find myself in Durban's mathematical grid of city-centre streets.

I'm staying on the seafront, so it's just a question of looking for the street with empty sky at the end of it. Easy. I'm there.

When I park in the Protea Balmoral backyard, a white security man takes details of the bike, my booking, myself . . . and promises me the BMW will be safe. 'There's twenty-four-hour security,' he says. 'White during the day, black after dark.'

Durban has an odd feel to it, the glamour of the Golden Mile – the Protea Balmoral is a grand old hotel, whose original 1908 staircase creaks in a ghostly fashion – descending just one street back into seediness and, frankly, strangeness. Elderly ex-surfers beg, and hotels for the retired abound. There's a pub called Thatcher's. Art deco architecture, grimy and uncared for, gives a hint of Miami beach. It's like Blackpool on steroids. No, Largs. Steroids cut with bad, bad shit.

It has taken me nine-and-a-half hours to cover the 578 miles from Port Alfred. I feel like I've gone fifteen rounds with Tyson at his peak, but at least my cold has gone. The room has the best air-conditioning I have ever encountered; it's like being in a fridge. I wonder about abandoning the trip, flying home from Durban, leaving the bike to be picked up. Crapping out. Instead, I drink a bottle of Chardonnay and fall asleep. Next morning, I feel better, slightly. I've survived the Transkei, after all. I haven't killed anyone. Not even myself.

I wonder what Mrs Johnson's funeral was like.

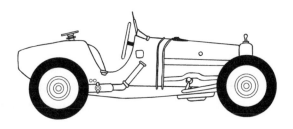

BEAUTIFUL FRIEND

'm ten, maybe eleven, and it's the pre-Christmas delivery run to relatives in the hinterlands of Glasgow and central Lanarkshire. Dad's driving a . . . what? I think this time it's a Fiat 125, the grey one he traded in for the Ford Executive. Or maybe it's the first of the Granadas.

Anyway, we've dropped off gifts, driving like motorised Santas from auntie to granny to uncle to cousin, and now we're moving out through Uddingston, one way or another coming home, I think. Or maybe going further into the satanic mills of the old industry. The road is dark. It's not a motorway. An ordinary, unlit road. We're overtaken by a motorcycle, travelling fast, thumping, roaring, snarling; probably a British bike. Moments later, the sky ahead is lit by a sudden orange glow, outlining a slight rise in the road. We drive on, the glow flickering, dying down, until we get to the top of the hill and there . . .

But, no, it didn't happen. I have never seen a motorcyclist lying in the road, ablaze, his petrol tank, possibly illegal alloy or plastic on a streetfighter special or café racer, a Triton or Norvil, split, explosive and fatal. It happened to Dad, though. He has never told me about it. But I did hear him describing the scene to my Uncle John.

Or maybe it was the other way round . . .

Since moving to Shetland, death has been a big part of my motoring experience. The islands' cavalier attitude towards the legalities of transportation has its dark side, and being married to a GP on twenty-four-hour accident and emergency call means that the destruction meted out by the internal combustion engine is often too close for comfort.

Medical confidentiality means that I have to be deliberately vague here, but I can mention the motorcycle accidents, ranging from the all-too-frequent and tragic loss of life to the living tragedy of a brilliant young guitarist losing the use of three fingers on his left hand and the wisecracking biker with a bit of femur sticking out through his leathers, who wanted to know if he'd have a romantic limp.

There are the quad-bike accidents, crush injuries from hillside manoeuvres gone wrong; the wildly drunk high-speed midnight chases which go awry, leaving boys dead, men embedded in peat bogs, hapless pedestrians mangled. And the everyday minor injuries, almost always involving alcohol, with the wrecked cars surreptitiously moved and hidden to avoid police attention.

Home.

For real ale in Surf City you have to drive out of town to the completely vast Westville Pavilion, a shopping centre so monstrous it makes LA's Beverley Mall look like a doll's supermarket. On the roof is the Firkin Hophouse Microbrewery, part of a chain which has shrunk in RSA but still thrives in the UK. It's a big, bustling, slightly uneasy place, halfway between a serious beer-drinker's howff and a sports bar. A toga party is advertised.

Albert, the brewer, is helpfulness itself, but I find the beers a bit of a mixter-maxter. Or a dog's breakfast, if you prefer. The Bishop's Bitter is excellent, hoppy and full-flavoured, but the pale ale is very strange, so pale it's lighter than any normal lager. The classic for me is Deuchar's India Pale Ale, that fearsome, dark-orange pint from Edinburgh. This is like water in comparison. The St Patrick's Millennium Porter is, as the name suggests, Irish and more like Beamish than Guinness – thinner, less bitter. The lager is more pungent than Castle, but is in the same mode.

Maybe it's my sinusitis. A curry might unblock them, I surmise, so off to the highly rated seafront Saagries I go. It's terrible, the mutton jaw-breakingly chewy, the spices vague and the flavours unresolved. Despite Durban being the curry capital of South Africa, this is the third bad one I've had in the city. Let me tell you, the best curries I've ever tasted have been in Glasgow and Wolverhampton. And once, curiously enough, in Salzgitter in Germany, a town built in the shape of a swastika, each road wide enough for two tanks to pass abreast.

Home.

My MZ, or MuZ Skorpion Sport, is yellow, like the BMW. In California, apparently, some BMW dealers have started selling Skorpions, and they are becoming cult bikes on the boulevards of LA. Big Thumpers, they call them. Single cylinder torque providers, vibrating sexily beneath your thighs, and groovy-looking as a Ducati. But much cheaper. And German.

MZ's story is an interesting one. On 13 April 1907 a Dane called Jorgen Rasmussen registered the warrant of establishment for an engineering works in the eastern German town of Zschopau. It was the start of an extraordinary business which would change the face of motorcycling technology worldwide, and a story of capitalism and communism, destruction and rebirth, betrayal, commitment, resilience and sheer mechanical brilliance.

Within twelve years of Rasmussen starting work, his company, DKW, was producing two-stroke engines of utter simplicity and amazing reliability. In 1922 production of the 150cc Reichsfahrtmodell began, one of the most successful motorcycle designs in history. Developed and refined over the following two decades, racing versions took European race tracks by storm, and in 1938 won the lightweight Isle of Man TT.

Then came war and, in its wake, several things happened. First, DKW's designs were appropriated as war reparations, and carbon-copy two-stroke motorcycles began appearing in both Britain – the legendary BSA Bantam – and America, where the makers of iron behemoths Harley Davidson decided the name Reichsfahrtmodel would never work in Des Moines, and called it the Hummer.

Later, when Japan's heavy industries began the long road to world domination, a small company called Yamaha cloned the DKW as well.

Meanwhile, Zschopau, and what had been the world's biggest motorcycle factory, was now firmly in East Germany, and while DKW re-established itself in the west, the state-owned Motorradwerk Zschopau (Zschopau Motorcycle Works), or MZ, was formed.

I know what you're thinking: ugly, smoky, two-stroke bikes which made a ring-a-ting-ting noise and were used from the late 1960s by a host of British commuters seeking cheap, reliable, unglamorous transport. Better than a CZ, even attracting a bit of a cult following in the late '70s and early '80s, but hardly a Suzuki. Well, thereby hangs a tale.

Throughout the late 1940s and '50s, MZ struggled, hopelessly underfunded, to make the brilliant designs of Walter Kaaden work on the road and on the race track. Prevented from competing on an equal footing by lack of finance and the ban on East German personnel entering certain countries, MZ's groundbreaking disc-valve two-strokes with tuned, resonating pressure-pulse exhausts were nevertheless almost unbeatable, when the team could get fuel, tools and spares.

Then came what is seen by many as betrayal. In 1961 MZ rider Ernst Degner was sitting at first place in the 125cc world championship, with only the Swedish round to go, when he defected, allegedly with the help of the Japanese, taking with him some of Walter Kaaden's secrets. Soon, Degner was riding for a company called Suzuki, who began making two-stroke racers using what appeared to be MZ's technology – technology which would dominate motorcycle racing for the following three decades.

INTERNAL COMBUSTION

170

Kaaden did not give up, using English rider Alan Shepherd and, previously unheard of, water-cooling to take the team to an overall third place in the world championships of 1964. Meanwhile, the blue smoke and ring-a-ting-ting of the basic road-going MZs spread across Europe and in particular the developing nations of Africa.

In 1973 a young medical student at Glasgow University was riding her TS150 all over Scotland and Ireland, before a horrific accident in Clydebank ended her motorcycling career, though not her affection for MZs. That was something she passed on to her husband, some fifteen years later. And so I found myself touring Scotland aboard an MZ ETZ250 combination, investigating, in the loosest sense of the word, whisky distilleries . . .

I sold the Orange Beast to a man in Campbeltown who wanted it for his pensioner mother to ride, but bought another ETZ three years later, a blue one. It reeked of character, and, in the wake of the Berlin Wall's collapse, I felt an oily nostalgia for the communist past which had produced it. Kind of radical kitsch-chic.

Back in Zschopau, it looked as if MZ were going to survive the reunification of Germany through their great historical strengths: brilliant design and innovation. Top British team Seymour-Powell was brought in and created one of the most beautiful motorcycle designs ever seen, the Skorpion. It looked like an instant classic, but the vast Zschopau factory seemed unable to make a go of producing it. MZ teetered on the edge of oblivion. Was eighty-five years of motorcycle manufacture in Zschopau to end?

Well, nearly. In 1992, a new company was formed, Motorrad und Zweiradwerk (Motorcycle and Two-wheeler Works), and drastic management surgery began. The remnant of the huge workforce was dismissed, the factory closed and all the manufacturing equipment, two-stroke designs and spares sold to a Turkish company. You can still buy ETZ301s and 250s today, built on the old Zschopau production lines, reassembled on the shores of the Mediterranean. They're called Kanunis. Some say they're better than ever.

MuZ nearly went under, but in the new internationalist climate of a united Germany were saved by investment from the Malaysian firm Hong Leon Industries. A new Zschopau factory, with a small, highly motivated eighteen-strong workforce and Japanese team-production techniques, all contributed to the sudden success of the Skorpion. An electric scooter is being produced, and a new twin-cylinder 125cc bike, the Kobra, is just out. It's got a motor designed by MuZ, instead of a Japanese parts-shelf special. I want one. Just for running around, you understand. Local trips to feed the sheep.

Two minibus taxis nearly sandwich me on the way out of Durban, heading for Johannesburg and home. This time it's the BMW's massive power which saves me, as opposed to its titanic braking ability. I wind back the throttle and, as the two combis glide together with me in the middle, I shoot out between the two of them like a cork from a shaken beer bottle.

Once out of Durban, the route regularises itself into a big, broad, remarkably quiet dual carriageway. Not quite motorway standard, but pretty damn close. This is the N3, and it's the best road I've been on yet in South Africa. By a long shot. I'm nervous about Johannesburg, with its fearsome reputation for violence, but before I'm far from Durban, just past Pietermaritzburg, I'm turning off into something which looks like a film set. For a middle-English idyll, circa 1950.

Chris Dean's Nottingham Road brewery is set on the stunning Rawdons fly-fishing estate in what's called the Midlands. The hotel is breathtaking, half-timbered, overgrown with lushness which looks not tropical but Kentish. The brewery is simply amazing. Chris is someone who has sorted out the fundamentals of brewing – that beer doesn't really travel, that it should cater for local trade, and that it should be made without compromise. The place is like an operating theatre.

If you ever get the chance, go to Rawdons. The bar in the hotel stocks all the beers and is the most conducive to quaffing that I saw in South Africa. There is a log fire when it is cold and the Pickled Pig Porter (pungent, no-compromise) is the ideal winter warmer. The Whistling Weasel pale ale is, thankfully, the real thing, and the Tiddly Toad Lager is a belter of a brew. Just down the road, also owned by Rawdons, is the Bierfassl, 'the All-Austrian Eating and Drinking Experience'. It's sausage a-go-go, but stick with the hotel bar. The brewery tour is conducted by Chris himself and is both informative and tasty. He's a bit fierce, though, in defence of his product. I can't tell you what he said about the Firkin in Durban, but the similarity between their labels and his is a matter of some, er . . . dispute.

I also have a feeling that bad things have happened here in the not too distant past. It's just too pretty, and there's something in Chris's voice when he talks about the downturn in tourism, the way that people are still afraid to come to the Midlands. It feels incredibly safe, but maybe appearances are deceptive.

Onwards on the N3, and I'm in Zulu territory. That's *Zulu* the movie. The mountains of the Drakensberg, or rather the amazing mushroom-shaped outcrops of rock, rise fungally from the green landscape until I'm climbing through the Drakensberg proper, through De Beers Pass, with diamonds in the air and an alpine influence on the architecture. You want Austria, you got Switzerland. After that it's a straight run into Jo'burg, the dirt in the air increasing, the smudge on the horizon gradually revealing its true monolithic, sprawling, solid mass.

In Jo'burg, and later in Mid Rand, I do radio interviews and tie up the details of the trip. I go out for a night's eating and drinking with Daniel, the *GQ* editor, and Julie, fashion editor, a black woman from London who travels everywhere with her car windows open and a Rolex on her arm in the firm belief that being black and confident will see her through any risk of mugging. 'I just talk to everybody,' she says, 'and I've never felt threatened in a whole year here. Never.'

Neither she nor I have ever eaten Nando's famous fried chicken, a South African phenomenon (actually, Portuguese-African) which has spread worldwide. So we find a little mall tucked away on the outskirts of Mid Rand where Julie attracts some odd looks. Or, rather, her dress, skin and the proximity of two white men does. Mid Rand is an enclave of whiteness. Julie, sussed daughter of Brixton that she is, shrugs it all off. Ignore it and it'll go away.

Except it won't. The chicken is disgusting. So we drink lots of Castle. It's fine, but nothing like the stronger stuff you get under the same name in Britain.

Back in the hotel bar, Daniel points out, quietly, the bulges under many arms. 'You and I are probably the only two men here who aren't carrying guns.' Makes nudging somebody a whole different proposition. Nobody except Julie is black.

Next day, my last, I have to take the BMW back to the company's South African HQ, where I am treated as if I have just crawled in from the gutter wearing a Chris Hani T-shirt and covered in elephant shit. Admittedly, the trusty BMW, with its crap gearchange but many, many life-saving plus points (basically, power and good brakes), is battered and filthy, but it's a press demonstrator, for goodness' sake. The two heavy-bellied Afrikaner executives in charge ignore me. They do not offer a lift back to the hotel, though I had been promised a ride to the airport. Their driver, who looks like a secret policeman from the De Klerk era, refuses point blank to take me. Maybe it's my body odour. Only the black secretary in the office takes pity on me and telephones my hotel for a courtesy bus to come and get me. This after refusing to countenance my walking back the half mile or so. It is, she says, unthinkable. I am too tired and fearful to argue.

The previous day, winding my way cautiously into the SABC headquarters in Jo'burg, a soaring, fascist skyscraper, I very nearly took the wrong turning into Hillbrow, famously the epicentre of the world murder capital. Its gangsters and drug-dealers have even become a tourist attraction for sick, thrill-seeking journos. I am not one of them. All I want now is for someone to look after me. And take me home. I want to stop moving. I want to stop. So I wait in the air-conditioned iciness of the BMW showroom, holding my helmet and thinking of the Heights Boys, and their marvellous Shetland garage-cum-cowshed. And wishing I was there, watching them bring a dying Hi-Lux back to life.

Garages are generally intimidating places full of people who hate you, who lurk under dead cars, unwilling to give you the time of day, and leave you hopping from foot to foot while your rubber-soled shoes melt into the oily concrete floor. A commercial radio station plays tinnily, breaking the first rule of garages in *Zen and the Art of Motorcycle Maintenance*: no distractions. When they finally deign to converse, these Swarfega-soaked engine-divers sneer openly at your ignorance, grunt insultingly, reluctantly agree to look at your vehicle a year hence and then charge you the price of a house for changing one spark plug.

At the current crop of American-influenced tyre and exhaust centres with names like *Phitphast*, *Clutchmelt* and *Stripbolt*, the policy pioneered by Kwik-Fit is at least partially in evidence: men dressed in very nearly clean nylon jumpsuits look you in the eye and occasionally smile. They will ask if they can help you, and even explain what it is they plan to do at vast expense to your charabanc. There will be a waiting area with magazines, an absence of girly calendars supplied by tyre manufacturers, and possibly some very bad coffee from a machine. True, these fast-fix drive-in emporiums of automotive reassurance usually do just tyres and exhausts, or, at a pinch, oil filters and clutches; those employed are not time-served mechanics. They are often not cheap at all. But they are easy and almost painless to frequent.

Not like real garages. My first experience as a potential, wheeled customer of a firm still operating on Glasgow's south side was of being told to go and get my father; then they would talk about fixing my Fiat 500. It must be said that my knowledge of how vehicles work has always left a lot to be desired, too, meaning that explanations of what needs sorted have been vague:

'There's a clunking noise . . .'

'Oh?'

'Yes, well, more of a . . . a clonk.'

'Or . . . a clank?'

'Yes! A clank!'

'Well, which is it? A clonk, a clunk or a clank?'

'Hmmm . . . a mixture of all three. Maybe with a bit of a clink as well, when you go round a sharp left-hander.'

When I lived in Glasgow, unable to afford anything but the most basic of rust-ridden transportation, I used to seek out railway-arch and hole-in-the-wall operations where MOTs would be torn off suspect pads with the embossed names of firms in Caithness, and where, on one occasion, the infamous Fiat 500 was driven by a not entirely sober mechanic through the back wall of the wooden shed being used as a workshop.

I would drive into one of these dens of iniquitous tinkering, navigating something decrepit like a Vauxhall Viva, a Hillman Avenger or an Austin 1100: 'It's stuttering/stammering/stopping/not starting,' I would tell the heid bummer, the mechanic with hair reeking of Castrol GTX and the face of an Easter Island statue sprayed with bunker fuel.

'Leave it with me,' he would mumble or grunt, and then, on my return, I would be met by a hissing intake of breath which seemed to last minutes, and a slow, sorrowful shaking of the head.

For a time I did my own basic servicing, which lent my one and only meeting with the legendarily waspish Muriel Gray, fifteen years ago, a surreal flavour of hydrocarbons. Having just serviced my pride and joy, a Fiat Mirafiori Twin-Cam, I set off down the A74 for Carlisle, there to interview Muriel (who was then doing a strange fashion and pop TV show called *Bliss* for Border TV) for *Melody Maker*. Accompanied by trusty snapper Stewart Cunningham, I reached Bothwell before the oil pressure warning light starting blinking. It was then I realised that my servicing had not included putting the oil filter seal on, and that there was a trail of Duckhams all the way from Maryhill. When we eventually met Muriel, an hour and a half late, she was pristine in white designer wear, while Stewart and I were both covered in oil from head to foot. To her everlasting credit, she voiced not a murmur of complaint and claimed to love Fiats. I had stopped liking them some hours previously.

These days, things are different. My contract-hired Peugeot came complete with a maintenance agreement. It's all easy. There's enough money to cope with proper garage demands. The one I deal with in Lerwick has no radio playing. And yet there is something liberating about running a sub-thousand-quid car, with a home-start RAC membership to take care of any little reliability blips. With the Heights Boys ready to come and sort out your troubles should anything disastrous occur, like total engine failure. And because they're neighbours, part of the community, they don't let you down. They are the *garagistes par excellence*. And, ironically, now I don't need to use them.

Unless I buy something cheap and old, for a bit of a laugh . . .

Ishmael looks after me. Call him Ishmael. After all, that's really his name. He drives a Toyota taxi, wears thin leather gloves and speaks hardly at all. He drives slowly, carefully, taking me back to the Protea from BMW, damn their eyes, and thence to Jo'burg International. It's almost over. He takes my generous tip and says goodbye, does Ishmael, but will not respond to my inquiries about traffic, violence, danger and politics. Who can blame him? 'We just want to get on with our lives,' is the most I can extract from him.

I leave South Africa behind, getting through passport control as quickly as possible, collapsing into the hoar-frost air-conditioned relief of departures. The duty-free section has been vastly enlarged. I buy nothing. No drinking. There's been too much drinking on this trip, and when I get home, after the flight to Amsterdam, the flight to Aberdeen and the flight to Shetland, the Land Rover is waiting. I'll have to drive.

I am not in love with my car, as Queen's Roger Taylor used to sing, and I do not intend to marry it. I have not been in love with any of my cars. I do not even lust after my wheels; when I used to watch the '80s TV series *Bergerac*, it was neither Jim Bergerac, his beautifully restored Riley (first of the great British telly detective cars, swiftly to be followed by Morse's Jaguar with its incredibly naff vinyl roof). But, then, it is hard to imagine anyone becoming passionate over a Peugeot 406 turbo-diesel, so basic it doesn't even have a rear wiper. It was a cheap lease, what can I tell you? Or a Land Rover. However, that is married love, not lust.

The 747 lifts into the air like a lump of the earth detaching itself. Impossible, this flight stuff. It can't be happening. It isn't real. I order a whisky. No more beer. Okay, I know I said I wasn't drinking, but it's nearly twenty hours before I'll be behind a wheel. Give me a break. I flick through the KLM in-flight magazine. There's a trivia section, a kind of *News of the Weird* rip-off. Over in Tennessee, there's this twenty-eight-year-old called Buster Mitchell, and he is giddy with automotive desire. He is more than infatuated, he is head over heels in obsessive love with his 1996 Ford Mustang GT, and he wants to marry it. Her. So far, even the liberal marital laws of Tennessee (thirteen-year-old cousins a speciality; see Lewis, Jerry Lee) have not relaxed sufficiently to allow conjugal bliss with a large lump of Detroit iron, and Buster has been left high and, so to speak, dry.

He is on the rebound, right enough, from his (human) girlfriend, who has just jilted him, probably out of jealousy. Buster doesn't see anything in the slightest bit odd about his relationship with a car, and claims it is far more normal than Californian same-sex marriages. Presumably he sees his car as female, which those who have noted the more usual phallic interpretation of the long, low, pointed shape of a Mustang's bonnet may find interesting. There is also the question of its name. A mustang is a lively male horse. Does Buster's car fixation betray something about his sexual nature that he has perhaps been unwilling to face up to? Is his car actually a man?

My relationship with the many cars I have owned has always been both simpler and more complex. The true petrolhead or diesel-daft dope, after all, knows that cars are not about sex at all. They are much more important than that. They are about freedom. Self-expression. Speed. Load-carrying capacity.

Or in my case, bargain hunting.

Once, I was obsessed with cheap cars or, if you will, bangers. The Viva with bald tyres, no windscreen wipers, no headlights and ubiquitous rust. When I was stopped by police on the M8, they couldn't speak for laughing. The Mitsubishi (then called a Colt – a young male horse, but don't read anything into it), with its aroma of cooking rotted kippers.

The Volvo 340 automatic, complete with daft DAF Dutch belt-drive gearbox, which was sold to two American birdwatchers who were later informed by a Volvo main dealer that they were driving a death trap. Amazingly, and fortuitously, it was stolen. The plastic-filled Lancia, £400 and worth maybe £20. But it looked great. The campers. Oh Lord, the campers . . .

It all got too much, and I moved on to safer, more reliable ground-covering gear. Hence the Peugeot. How can I tell you how boring it was? It started first time, every time, ran perfectly, had a great stereo, comfortable seats, and the door hinges never squeaked.

No wonder I had to get rid of it.

No, waiting for me now at Sumburgh is the end of my motoring road. Vast, upright, solid and British. Functional in the extreme. Everlasting. Slow, yes, but reliable and, in a perverse way, fantastic fun. All I want, all I need. All I will ever need.

Honest.

I wake up at some godless hour of the night–morning, the whole aeroplane like a mobile refugee camp, all huddled, blanketed figures, food detritus on the floor, uniformed guards making sure we stay in line, queues for the toilets, which are filthy and blocked. KLM is worse than British Airways, and I never thought I'd say that about any airline. I have been dreaming of motorcycles, and the throbbing in my arms reminds me how much pain has gone into riding the BMW some two thousand African miles. And how little insight I've gained into South Africa, one of the most important countries, politically, on earth.

Hey, it was a quick trip, I tell myself, and I was on a straight commission from a magazine which wanted something precise, no politics: it was about beer and bikes, and was thus superficial and stupid. And probably worthless. Apart from the several hundred quid I'm getting from *GQ* for writing about it. It might just pay for the bulletproof vest I've never worn.

Schiphol is a pain in the feet, involving miles of trudging to the gate for Aberdeen. At Aberdeen I'm comprehensively turned over by customs, who eye my tattered passport with disapproval. 'Why,' asks one officer, 'couldn't the magazine have used a South African journalist?'

God knows, I reply.

Turbo-propping into Shetland, I hit the ground and feel the sweeping, lung-opening cold of the saltiest of salt winds. As ever, I feel like kissing the tarmac, like a would-be secular pope.

In the arrivals hall at Sumburgh, I glimpse my wife. What's wrong, I wonder. She's meant to be waiting at home. We embrace. No kids are there. They're at school, I remember. What's wrong?

'I've got some bad news,' she says. 'There's been an accident.'

God, no. Is it one of the children? My sisters? My father?

'Apparently a JCB was digging out a ditch at the airport car park when it ran out of control, and it . . . hit your Land Rover. It's completely written off . . . I know how much you loved that car . . .'

A great wave of relief breaks over me. A realisation dawns almost instantly. I can buy a new car with a completely clear conscience! Fantastic news!

'It happened just after you left, so in fact the insurance people have moved really quickly, and we're going to pick up the replacement from the boat on the way back. Same colour, same interior finish, same everything! Isn't that great?'

The truth is that I often lie to my wife about cars and how I feel about them. It's a type of adultery, only in metal, and mobile. But until this moment, I hadn't realised how much I lie to myself. Because when she said that the Land Rover had been written off, those old Lamborghini dreams came flocking in, glowing, curvy, all-consuming.

'I got a taxi down, but we might as well get the bus back to Lerwick,' she says. 'Bet you can't wait to see how your new Land Rover measures up to the old one.'

'That's right, dear,' I murmur, embracing her, heart heavy, smiling manically. 'I can't.'

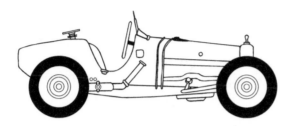

THE LAST, LAST CAR

t's over. I promise you, I have finished this obsessive buying and selling of cars, this use of machinery as metaphor. I have my motorbikes. And now I have the Last Car. Well, it's a sort of car. At least it's not a Peugeot. Or, saints preserve us, a Citroën. This is, accidentally, Land Rover Number Two. Meet the old boss, same as the new boss. I have buried the Lamborghini dreams beneath delight in beginning my Land Rover life again from zero on the odometer.

Men and motors. *Men and Motors*: it's the name of that rather unappetising, testosterone-soaked digital television channel; and it's a deep, central truth of human existence. For many males, cars are life and, sad as that may seem, the measuring out of one's time on earth in terms of vehicles owned is as natural as eating or breathing. To move, after all, as I have tried to argue, is to live.

Here I am, in my mid-forties. I can conjure up whole chunks of my childhood by naming a car and inhaling its imagined, memorised aroma: a Wolseley, two-tone blue over grey, its leather seats and carpeted floor bedspace for my two sisters and me. The plasticky, hot-clutch smell of a Vauxhall Cresta, broken down with a ruined universal joint in Lyon. The utterly distinctive polystyrene pong of every Fiat my family owned, and which every new product of Turin still possesses: spinning my father's 131 Sport on the Ayr bypass; splitting my head open when my Fiat 500 crashed into a stationary car on St Andrew's Drive; the infectious weirdness of my mother's robot-built Fiat Strada. Hundreds of memories. Thousands of triggers for nostalgia.

As for my own custodianship of various wheeled machines, there's no question that my entire existence can be described in terms of in-car events: that first kiss, cigarette, rejection of God, rejection by innumerable women, jobs, journeys, joys and sorrows. MGs, Renaults, Lancias, Volvos, Fords, Volkswagens . . . the list goes on and on. Peugeots. But that was only leased. Next I'll be counting hired cars, and that could get very complicated indeed.

Now the love affair with automobiles is over, for I have truly reached the beginning of the end of the road. No longer will I lust after Aston Martins, Lamborghinis, Jaguars or other extreme examples of automotive artistry. I would like to say that it's an environmental thing, but it isn't. Finally, you abandon the car as fantasy, as dream machine, and embrace it as nothing more or less than a practical tool. The Peugeot – repmobile, utterly innocuous, good at its job except for the fact that it never, ever de- misted properly in rain – was a last step on the road to where I am now. Before it, the Volvo was a significant purchase too.

However, in my case, it so happens that the purchase of a vehicle where form follows function to an almost ridiculous extent is a dream come true. Because the truth is that from the day I was given a Dinky Toy version, I have yearned for a Land Rover.

The Dinky was grey, a model of the Series One or Two 88-inch hard- top. What I have now, for the second time, is a Rioja red Defender 110 Station Wagon County TDI, complete with an unbelievable twelve seats, aluminium bodywork which ripples and bends in a strangely appealing way, a viable cruising speed of 65 mph (any more and the North Sea runs dry of oil within a week). It can handle dogs, grannies, teams of children, hay, pigs, sheep, hen food and large amounts of gravel, all with ease and aplomb. Its permanent four-wheel drive deals easily with the vicissitudes of the Shetlandic roadscape. And, best of all, it is utterly itself. A Land Rover is a Land Rover is a Land Rover, and is recognisably the same machine made for farmers more than half a century ago. It is a classic in a way a Toyota Landcruiser or Mitsubishi Shogun could never be. Even the recent use of the name 'Defender' is meant to inflame purchasers with pride in the British forces' use of Land Rovers for everything from fire engines to long-range desert assault vehicles. And there they were on the front line in Sierra Leone, on the news. I feel happy in a Land Rover; I feel safe. I feel at home.

After I came home from South Africa, after the second Land Rover had become part of the family, BMW announced it was pulling out of Rover and indeed had sold Land Rover to Ford, while the question of what happened to the Cowley plant and all who work there remained very unclear indeed. Land Rover – profitable, competitive, internationally prestigious – was the jewel in the Rover Group's crown. But for the family-dominated BMW, the going was just too tough. As the whole car manufacturing industry worldwide becomes concentrated in the hands of a few multinationals (Volvo is now part of Ford, Saab has gone with General Motors and GM even have a shareholding in the Agnelli family's once mighty Fiat), BMW are just not big enough to cope. Ford, on the other hand, know exactly what they are doing, have cherry-picked the best names and the most valuable products – from the Jaguar XK8 to the Range Rover – and even the plug ugly, venerable but still enormously saleable Defender is safe under their ownership.

The truth is that what BMW get from Ford will help to cover the massive costs of handing over the rest of the group, save of course the new Mini, to all the uncertainties of the Phoenix Consortium. In some ways, it's surprising that Ford didn't just snap up BMW. After all, there's a shared Nazi past, with Ford subsidiaries involved in building vehicles for Germany under Hitler, even after America went to war. At the end of the conflict, Ford went so far as to demand compensation for damage done to its German premises by Allied bombers.

The Land Rover I own was built under BMW's regime, and is reputedly all the better for it. Which is to say, it works. Even when Honda was disgustingly gazumped by the Bavarian firm in buying Rover, there was fury from some harrumphing quarters at the idea of the British Rover falling under foreign – worse, German – control. Not so much control as quality control; the post-1994 Land Rovers are much better than the older models. Now, the absorption of Land Rover into Ford is causing less angst among enthusiasts. Ford have allowed Aston Martin and Jaguar to operate as independently as anyone could have hoped, with the advantage of access to a worldwide stockholding of engineering expertise and parts. Which is why you hear people talking about a Jaguar which is just a Mondeo in drag, or a DB7 which uses two Ford engines stuck together. But, as I've said, Ford have lots of experience of arm's-length operating arrangements with companies they own in foreign lands . . .

There are only two wholly owned all-British manufacturing car companies left, and those are TVR and Morgan. Only TVR build their own engines, and it was their specialised sports car niche which was one of the inspirations for the original Alchemy bid for Rover. But that is really all that is left to the one-country car-maker now: niches. Everybody wants a niche. But if your niche gets too big, the multinationals will want to move in. In the nicest possible way, of course, preserving as many vestiges of national pride and historic iconography as they feel suits their financial purpose.

A few weeks after the BMW announcement, after the collapse of the Alchemy bid and the desperate transfer of everything Roverish (except Land Rover) to the cobbled-together Phoenix consortium, plus millions of quid for their trouble, Ford announced that it was closing its Dagenham plant. Oh yes, they might be able to take Land Rover, its products, technology and image, and start churning out Freelanders in Taiwan or Vietnam, but there was nothing iconographic about Dagenham, nothing saleable. Well, not for Ford. 'Dagenham Dave' badges and 'Demarcation Agreement' sweatshirts don't have much of a market these days. Fiestas can be made anywhere. Stuff Dagenham. Save Solihull, home of the Land Rover. Let's take our revenge on the community which caused us all that grief for all those years.

Heil!

But I have a Land Rover, not a Fiesta. I am driving an icon. And its future is secure, even it does become foreign in the long run.

'A gentleman's conveyance,' said an acquaintance, somewhat sneeringly, on seeing the gigantic shape of my Land Rover in his car park. I felt strangely warmed. Despite all the alterations in overall ownership of the firm, I even experienced some degree of national pride. After all, the British designed the Land Rover. Just look at it: it's got Britishness written all over it.

Except, of course, it's really just a ripped-off Jeep, cobbled together after the war and based on the hundreds of former US Army vehicles left in Blighty. So after all this, now that Land Rover is American, maybe it's going home at last. As for my Rioja red monster, it smells of new rubber and old dog and abandoned fags, diesel and silage. I hope the kids won't merely have to imagine that niff when they grow up, either; for, unlike BMW, I don't intend to sell.

I will keep moving, though. At a steady, legal 60 mph, being frugal with diesel, being responsible, making sure the kids are all securely belted in.

And if I want to scare myself silly, I'll have a menopausal trip on one motorbike or another, leaning into corners as the back end of the MZ wobbles, scraping along the thrilling edge of imminent death or paralysis or ignominious skiting along the gravel and into the peat. I'll watch *Top Gear* on the telly, and wait for the moment when the children are old enough to want their own transportation. I'll attempt to talk them out of motorbikes, help them search for second-hand cars, pay for them, pray for them, repair them, nag them about looking after the things properly. They'll get faster; I'll slow down.

Until one day, I'll be popped in a box in the back of a custom-built black Ford hearse, if nobody listens to my own daft request that they put me in a sack in the back of the Land Rover, for the last journey, at a snail's pace, to the seaside cemetery next to our croft. And there I'll stop. The cars and bikes will rot. And so will I.

You won't believe this: somebody is advertising a limited-edition Jaguar XJ8 in the paper. New £55,000, selling for £12,000. And it's local. Just down the road. Full service history. Unique colour scheme, silver over black...

Get thee behind me, Satan!

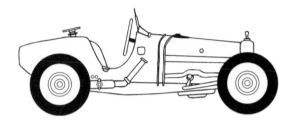

EDITOR'S NOTE

s *Internal Combustion* was being prepared for press, the following incoherent e-mail was received from Tom Morton. As Mr Morton was under contract to this publisher, it was decided to continue with the publication of the book. But in the interests of truth and accuracy, this letter is also printed, though without comment.

Deborah,

Sorry. I tried, as hard as I could to resist, to maintain the integrity of the book's structure, and to remain true to my own auto-motive vows.

But yesterday I met this fisherman from the island of Whalsay, and he was getting rid of his 1981 Merecedes 280SE. That's the W126 body, the last of the truly great Mercs, and fitted with one of the all-time brilliant engines, the Mercedes-Benz straight 2.8 six. It's a rusty big hulk, but it's MOTd for nearly a year and taxed for four months. It's painted Nordic Blue, the same as the variety of dead parrot in the Monty Python sketch, but that's not important right now. This is important: I bought it. For £700. Seven hundred quid. And it runs like an air-conditioned, fully enclosed flying carpet. It has done a mere 134,000 miles, with these Merc engines bench-tested to half a million, and the

Mercedes three-pointed star. And it's at least two feet longer than most cars on the road. Most other large cars.

Of course, it only runs on four-star petrol, which you can't get, and then only does about sixteen miles per gallon. But when you're in it, whirring down a long staight, cruise control set, it makes the Land Rover seem like a tractor. It's indulgent, it's impractical. It's even ridiculous, in this environmentally friendly age. But in it, surrounded by that strange Merc wood finish, lolling giant armchair seats, you feel like a million dollars. For £700.

I'm not abandoning the Land Rover. The Merc will break, or become unrepairable, or be stored away, probably within the year. It's a kind of unfaithfulness, I suppose; an affair. But then, I found out some stuff about the second Land Rover. It seems the mileage was wrong, and the full service history has mysteriously vanished. So I don't feel too guilty.

The Pope once owned a Merc like mine, you know.

Anyway, don't mention this to anyone. Let the book stand in its own right as a statement at the time it was written. I mean, there's literature. And then there's the feeling you get when that engine gets thumped into kickdown and you surge past everything in front of you in virtual silence. There's no contest, really.

Yours sincerely,

Tom Morton

Strasburg, France